Powerful Practices

for

HIGH-PERFORMING
Special Educators

ROBERTA KAUFMAN
ROBERT WANDBERG

CORWIN
A SAGE Company

For information:

Corwin
A SAGE Company
2455 Teller Road
Thousand Oaks, California 91320
(800) 233-9936
Fax: (800) 417-2466
www.corwin.com

SAGE Ltd.
1 Oliver's Yard
55 City Road
London EC1Y 1SP
United Kingdom

SAGE India Pvt. Ltd.
B 1/I 1 Mohan Cooperative Industrial Area
Mathura Road, New Delhi 110 044
India

SAGE Asia-Pacific Pte. Ltd.
33 Pekin Street #02-01
Far East Square
Singapore 048763

Printed in the United States of America

Library of Congress Cataloging-in-Publication Data

Kaufman, Roberta Brack.
Powerful practices for high-performing special educators/Roberta Kaufman, Robert Wandberg.
    p. cm.
Includes bibliographical references and index.
ISBN 978-1-4129-6807-2 (pbk.)
   1. Children with disabilities—Education. 2. Special education teachers. I. Wandberg, Robert. II. Title.

LC4015.K38 2010
371.9′043—dc22   2010001674

This book is printed on acid-free paper.

10 11 12 13 14   10 9 8 7 6 5 4 3 2 1

Acquisitions Editor:	Jessica Allan
Associate Editor:	Joanna Coelho
Editorial Assistant:	Allison Scott
Production Editor:	Amy Schroller
Copy Editor:	Nancy Conger
Typesetter:	C&M Digitals (P) Ltd.
Proofreader:	Eleni Georgiou
Indexer:	Michael Ferreira
Cover Designer:	Karine Hovsepian

Contents

Publisher's Acknowledgments

Corwin gratefully acknowledges the contributions of the following reviewers:

Rachel Aherns, Level 1 Special education teacher
Westridge Elementary School, West Des Moines, IA

Renee Bernhardt, Special education teacher
Florine Dial Johnston Elementary, Woodstock, GA

Dawne Dragonetti, Special education teacher, Grades 3–5
Center School, Stow, MA

Alison Martins, Special education teacher
Seven Hills Charter Public School, Worcester, MA

Mary Reeve, Special education director
Gallup-McKinley County Public Schools, Gallup, NM

Betty Rivinus, Principal
Baker Prairie Middle School, Canby, OR

Nancy Yost, Professor
Indiana University of Pennsylvania, Teacher Education Center, Indiana, PA

About the Authors

Roberta Kaufman has been a P–12 special educator and university administrator in the Midwest where she has worked in both rural and urban settings. Her professional experience includes coordinating a partnership between multiple school districts in a metropolitan area and a university to design and implement a teacher preparation program for underrepresented populations. Dr. Kaufman initiated a program providing instructional seminars followed by coaching support for individuals hired as special educators in a diverse urban school district. Practices described in Powerful Practices for High-Performing Special Educators were implemented throughout the seminars and observed in classrooms with follow-up coaching. As a result of the coaching and seminars, a dramatic increase in the retention of new special education teachers was documented and maintained beyond two years. She is currently on the faculty of the School of Education at the University of South Dakota.

Robert Wandberg currently serves as the Language Diverse Literacy Coach for the Columbia Heights School District in Minnesota. His responsibilities include providing classroom teachers with effective, best-practice strategies for working with English language learners, special education students, and low-literacy learners. He is a former middle and high school classroom teacher and state curriculum specialist with the Minnesota Department of Education. In addition to his numerous state, national, and international presentations, Dr. Wandberg has authored 12 middle and high school level textbooks for low-literacy students. He has also coauthored two university-level textbooks focusing on effective classroom practice, as well as several professional journal articles, many of which focus on diverse students in the general education classroom. He also teaches graduate education courses at Minnesota State University, Mankato.

Introduction

Stories special educators tell of their immersion into the profession are often told in disbelief that they beat the odds. Pathways to becoming a special educator are some of the most varied in the profession.

Retention of special educators is an issue that has been a concern and has been wrestled with for at least two decades. Whether a person stays or leaves teaching is often dependent on more than one factor, but among reasons given for exiting the profession are academic training, level of support provided by administrators, understanding of roles and responsibilities, feelings of collegiality with other teachers in the building, facilities and available resources, caseloads, paperwork, and student behavior.

Costs associated with the continual turnover of special education teachers are considered a burden to school districts that invest in the recruitment of special education teachers.

When Madelyn Will (1986) considered the question "What's so special about special education?" the elephant in the room was revealed. Educational experiences that students with disabilities had been receiving were a product of a dual system. The precedent established in Brown versus the Board of Education that "separate is not equal" has been pivotal in promoting the concept that the academic welfare of students with disabilities is the responsibility of all educators.

Rather than serving as a faucet that is used to release pressure when the steam is too hot, special education should be designed as a finely tuned instrument that is selected carefully by professionals who are relentless and intentional in their commitment to teach all students. With the heightened emphasis on student achievement, now, more than ever, it is necessary to have highly effective special education teachers using research-based instructional practices with students on individual education programs (IEPs). The revolving door of special education teachers leaving the profession does little to enhance the academic integrity and continuity of a student's program.

Teacher education programs are being asked to guarantee their graduates will be able to ensure and document a year of progress in student achievement. Most administrators and principals who hire and support new special educators know they must encourage and provide professional development. Confident, competent, and connected special education teachers apply knowledge and use their secure skills but also recognize areas where they can improve.

Topics in this book were selected because they were identified by new special educators and best-practice research as the most necessary practices in becoming a successful special education teacher. Contemporary research and focused observations of novice special educators confirmed the need for specific skills and knowledge in order to survive and thrive in the early years of one's career.

Chapter 1, *Working with Diverse Students,* is unique from the other chapters because it addresses the changing population of students that all teachers need to be prepared to educate. It is an overview of one factor among many that must be addressed in the complex task of meeting the needs of diverse students in the world of special education. The nitty-gritty issues presented in Chapter 2, *Organizing a Classroom for Instruction,* and Chapter 3, *Managing Student Behavior,* are front and center in the minds of new special education teachers. Ideas from these chapters can be adapted and used to provide a basis to research other effective practices specific to a teacher's classroom setting.

Once some level of order is achieved, the art of teaching becomes a priority. Chapter 4, *Designing Effective Instruction;* Chapter 5, *Teaching Strategies and Learning Activities;* Chapter 6, *Graphic Organizers;* Chapter 7, *Incorporating Technology,* and Chapter 8, *Student Assessment and Evaluation,* describe effective instructional practices to be used in the educational setting. The final chapter, *Promoting Achievement Through Collaboration,* affirms that successful teachers rely on partnerships as a fundamental and ongoing component of instruction.

Each chapter provides examples of situations a special educator faces daily. More importantly, the chapters contain classroom and instructional suggestions for new special education teachers to implement immediately. The strategies come from the research and have been implemented by highly effective teachers to support student achievement.

To achieve the book's purpose, all chapters contain examples of teaching practices designed for instructional success. The chapters each list the Spanish and Hmong word for the number as a reminder to think inclusively. Each chapter begins with **Chapter Objectives**. The chapter objectives describe what the reader will know and/or be able to do as a result of conscientious reading. Next, the **Chapter Introduction** briefly provides the reader with the focus and essence of the chapter. The **Wisdom of Practice** section bonds the chapter objectives to a real-life educational practice that allows for an additional chapter focal point. What about the research supporting the chapter's targeted educational practices? The **In Brief: What Does the Research Say?** section describes the best-practices research that substantiates the chapter's content. **Chapter Summaries** provide a brief chapter review. The **Self-Assessment and Reflection** allows the reader to reflect and self-test the chapter's information. And, finally, the **Reference** list provided at the end of the book lists the many useful references found throughout each chapter.

Use this book in the following ways:

1. As a daily resource. Pull it off the shelf regularly to add to your teaching practices.

2. As a tool for professional development. Focus on one chapter a month throughout the year.

3. As a training document for preservice teachers ready to enter the profession. Provide it as a text for student teaching seminars.

4. As a discussion point for collaboration in the school. Bring staff together to initiate the use of consistent strategies.

5. As a guide for those whose quick entry into the arena of special education found them underprepared. Give it as a gift of support.

6. As a refresher for experienced regular and special education teachers needing new ideas. Generate divergent thinking.

7. As a model of integrated practices that support all learners. Document the successes.

8. As a textbook in college and university courses such as Student Teaching Seminar, Special Education Practicum, Inclusive Practices, Differentiating Instruction, Research and Practice in Special Education, Teaching Diverse Learners, Instructional Practices for Students with Disabilities, and Special Education Methods and Materials.

1

one—uno—ib

Working With Diverse Students

OBJECTIVES

1. Discuss the changing student diversity and demographics.

2. Describe the impact of diverse populations in special education programming.

3. Incorporate effective strategies associated with achievement of diverse students with disabilities.

4. Use the What Works Clearinghouse to identify and provide examples of effective instructional programs.

5. Compare and contrast the cultural context of disabilities associated with diverse populations.

6. Dispel myths associated with teaching diverse students with disabilities.

7. Analyze personal skills and competencies to increase effectiveness in working with diverse students with disabilities.

Special education teachers have responsibility for an increasingly diverse student population. Over- and underrepresentation of certain populations on Individual Education Programs (IEPs) are concerns in many schools. Special education referrals and census data of diverse students including English language learners (ELLs) present a complex and often confusing picture. Cultural background and belief systems impact the view some families have about disabilities.

Chapter 1 provides an overview of the changing demographics and cultural influences students bring to the classroom. In addition, the chapter identifies professional and instructional practices known to be effective with diverse students before and during referral, as well as after diagnosis of a disability.

WISDOM OF PRACTICE:
THE TECHNICOLOR WORLD OF TRUMAN ARMSTRONG

Of the 16 names on Truman Armstrong's special education caseload, he could barely pronounce 11. Truman read through the list, stopping as he tried to pronounce some of the names, "Anderson, Assad, Carlson, Harris, Juarez, LaPointe, Martinez, Nelson, Nguyen, Thao, Vallejo, Vasquez, Wilson, Xiong, Yusuf, Zupinski." He certainly had not expected such diversity when he returned to his rural hometown to begin his first year of teaching. Thinking back on some of the courses he had taken, Truman remembered that language and opportunity to learn could be misperceived by educators. He wondered if the students really belonged in special education. Truman looked for the students' files. Some of the files were incomplete and others were vague. Thoughts were racing in his mind. "What are the backgrounds of the students? Do they speak English? I don't speak ANY foreign language . . . well, German, maybe, when my grandmother is around! Is there an ELL teacher?" Truman started to make a list of questions and people to talk to.

Like Truman Armstrong, special education teachers face rapidly changing student demographics. Special educators are able to increase their effectiveness and confidence when they use strategies known to be instructionally powerful with diverse students who have special education needs. Student achievement can be enhanced when cultural and linguistic backgrounds are addressed.

IN BRIEF: WHAT DOES THE RESEARCH SAY?

Diversity includes gender, race, culture, language, religion, age, socioeconomic status, geographic location, sexual orientation, and ability or disability. Cultural and linguistic variables can be particularly challenging in special education referrals, assessment, and instruction.

Changing Student Diversity

Student demographics reflect the changes in society as a whole. Demographics vary dramatically by geographic location, but the average classroom of 30 students would typically have 15 Caucasian, 8 African American, 5 Latino/a, 1 Asian/Pacific Islander, 1 Native American, and 1 "other" student. Of those 30 students in the class, 4 would be identified with disabilities, 2 with specific learning disabilities, 1 with cognitive disabilities, and 1 with emotional behavior disorders. Six of the 30 students would be non-English speakers.

Language

Approximately 20 percent of students aged 5–17 speak a home language other than English, and nearly four million students in the United States are ELLs (United States Department of Education, 2006). The following are the most common language groups:

Language	Approximate Percentage
1. Spanish	77.0
2. Vietnamese	2.4
3. Hmong	1.8
4. Korean	1.2
5. Arabic	1.2
6. Haitian Creole	1.1
7. Cantonese	1.0
8. Tagalog	.9
9. Russian	.9
10. Navajo	.9
11. All others	11.8

Race

The National Center for Educational Statistics (NCES) in *The Condition of Education* (2008) identified 43 percent of the student population in the United States as being non-Caucasian, over 10 million nationwide. The increase of culturally and linguistically diverse students reinforces the need for teachers to be knowledgeable of family practices, values, and resources that students with a global history bring to school. This book is designed to support a more inclusive perspective.

THE IMPACT OF DIVERSE POPULATIONS IN SPECIAL EDUCATION PROGRAMMING

In 2004, the *Descriptive Study of Services to Limited English Proficient (LEP) Students and LEP Students with Disabilities* (Zehler, Fleishman, Hopstock, Stephenson,

Pendzick, et al,. 2004) reported approximately 357,325 ELLs (or 9.2 percent of the student population) were provided special education services. This was the first national estimate of ELLs served under Individuals with Disabilities Education Act (IDEA). Child Count data from the United States Department of Education (2006) indicated that the number of ELLs who are on IEPs may be as high as 20 percent of the total special education population.

Disproportionate Representation

Disproportionate representation, high dropout rates, and the achievement gap for minority and culturally and linguistically diverse students remain concerns for special educators. Disability areas where Hispanic, Black, and Native American students are overrepresented include specific learning disabilities, cognitive impairment, and emotional behavioral disorders (Artiles & Trent, 1994; Duany & Pittman, 1990, Harry & Klingner, 2005; Zehr, 2004). Among native races in the United States, American Indian and Alaska Native populations have been reported as having some of the highest percentage of disabilities—22 percent, according to the 2000 Federal Census (Ogunwole, 2002). As many as 12.2 percent of African Americans are reported to have the most severe disabilities, in comparison with Asian/Pacific Islanders, the lowest reporting group, with 4.9 percent reporting severe disabilities (Kraus, Stoddard, & Gilmartin, 1996).

Teacher Attitude

In a 2002 study, Carlson, Brauen, Klein, Schroll, and Willig found that special education teachers self-reported feeling least skillful in working with ELL students with disabilities. Critical obstacles to culturally responsive teaching include negative teacher attitudes and expectations for students of color, and confusing disability with diversity (Gay, 2002). According to some researchers, there is an urgent need to refine the theoretical framework and methodologies used in preservice teacher education programs in order to better prepare general and special educators to work with diverse students and study the impact of multicultural students (Trent & Artiles, 1998).

Teacher Preparation

Preparation of special education teachers to meet the needs of ELLs is an area gaining attention in order to ensure effective assessment and instruction. Many programs that proliferated with the help of federal funds in the 1980s have been restructured or eliminated. Currently, fewer than 15 bilingual special education programs exist in the United States (Paneque & Barbetta, 2006). Although special education professional standards require knowledge and skill in language development, communicating with ELL students, and distinguishing between language difference and language disability, the competencies of teachers are just beginning to catch up to the needs of a growing student population.

PROFESSIONAL PRACTICE

Special education teachers have a responsibility to be aware of and sensitive to the needs of diverse learners as well as to provide them with an appropriate education.

Special Education Teacher
Competencies When Working With ELL Students

The following competencies have been identified as necessary when working with ELL special education students (Baca and Amato, 1989):

1. Desire to work with culturally and linguistically exceptional children

2. Ability to work effectively with parents of ELL students

3. Ability to develop an appropriate IEP

4. Knowledge and sensitivity toward the language and culture of the group served

5. Ability to teach English as a second language

6. Ability to conduct nonbiased assessment with culturally and linguistically exceptional students

7. Ability to use appropriate methods and materials when working with ELLs

Other knowledge and skills that special educators find helpful to work successfully with ELL special education students include the following:

1. Awareness of the scope of multicultural issues, including those that are medical, economic, religious, social, and political

2. Knowledge of the stages of language development and use

3. Willingness to collaborate

4. Skill in identifying and utilizing school and community resources for culturally and linguistically diverse students with special needs

5. Knowledge of the impact of the physical environment

6. Ability to identify stress factors

7. Fluency in a second language

Given the number of languages spoken in schools, it may be rare to speak the student's native language or be from the same culture, however, sensitivity is important.

Culturally responsive special education is advocated by Geneva Gay as a comprehensive endeavor that will positively impact diagnosing students' needs, curriculum content, counseling and guidance, instructional strategies, and performance assessment (Gay, 2002). Gay calls for a mix of "tough love" and unequivocal caring that translates into an emotionally safe and supportive place where the standard of achievement is challenging but set within reasonable and reachable levels. Multiple opportunities should be provided so students can be successful. Creative and imaginative methods, including the use of technology, are critical for engaging students who might be considered hard to teach. In order to eliminate bias, reduce stereotypes, and increase the chances of a more desirable living and learning climate, Gay promotes engaging students in activities that incorporate social justice and service learning.

The importance of effective strategies and research-based instructional methods and programs should not be underestimated. Practices selected because they are appropriate for the learner will reinforce student achievement when used consistently.

Effective Strategies and Student Achievement for Diverse Learners

The Institute of Education Sciences established by the United States Department of Education hosts the What Works Clearinghouse (WWC), found at http://ies.ed.gov/ncee/wwc/. The WWC lists and rates scientifically based instructional practices. The Web site is a helpful resource that special education teachers can access when making decisions about what methods are valid and reliable for diverse special education students.

For English language learners, peer tutoring pairs and response groups were two practices that received the highest rating of effectiveness for English language development (WWC, 2008). The rating is based on "positive effects" and "strong evidence of a positive effect with no overriding contrary evidence." In other words, these are practices that should be used. Peer tutoring pairs involves one student tutoring the other, who needs the additional support to reinforce learning. Response groups typically involve four or five students working together and sharing responsibility to complete a task. Both tutoring pairs and response groups emphasize the use of peer interaction and discussion to complete a task.

Other researchers have added to the field of ELL special education best practices. In their study, *Educator Perceptions of Standards-Based Instruction for English Language Learners With Disabilities,* Thurlow, Albus, Shyyan, Liu, and Barerra (2004) noted strategies that have been found to support reading, math, and science achievement. Listed opposite are 12 strategies special educators have rated as highly effective in reading, math, and science.

WHAT WORKS? AN ACTIVITY

Read through the list of 12 strategies below. Select the five strategies you believe are most successful for reading. Then select five for math and five for science. Identify only five strategies (no more, no less) for each of the three content areas. Some of the strategies may have more than one letter. On the line in front of the strategy, write R for reading, M for math, and S for science. The answers will be provided later in the chapter.

_____ 1. Cooperative Learning

Students work as a team to accomplish a task

_____ 2. Curriculum-Based Probes

Student performance of skills that are timed and then charted to reflect growth

_____ 3. Direct Teaching of Vocabulary

Specific vocabulary instruction using a variety of activities that hold attention

_____ 4. Explicit Timing

Timing of seatwork to increase proficiency

_____ 5. Graphic Organizers

Visual display of information to structure concepts and ideas

_____ 6. Peer Tutoring

Pairing students, with one trained to tutor the other

_____ 7. Preassessment Organization Strategies

Use of specific practices designed to reinforce student's recall of content

_____ 8. Reciprocal Peer Tutoring

Pairing students who then select a team goal and tutor each other

_____ 9. Specific Informal Assessments

Use of a variety of methods including questioning for retention

_____ 10. Teacher Think-Alouds

Explicit steps are modeled out loud in order to develop steps in problem solving processes

_____ 11. Using Short Segments to Teach Vocabulary

Short time segments are used to teach vocabulary through listening, speaking, reading, and writing

_____ 12. Using Response Cards During Instruction

Students write brief answers to teacher questions and hold them up so teacher can review answers

A number of these practices are incorporated in programs that have also been researched and found valuable for student achievement. As with any instructional strategy or educational program, the age, background, and needs of the student must be taken into consideration.

Highly Effective Reading Programs

According to the WWC, the following programs and methods had positive effects on reading achievement:

1. *Bilingual Cooperative Integrated Reading and Composition (BCIRC) ***

BCIRC is a bilingual program that uses cooperative groups during instruction that focus on reading, writing, and speaking. Instructional practices are not watered down but develop social, academic, and communication skills consistent with the developmental level of students. See www.cal.org/resources/digest/cooperation.html.

2. *Enhanced Proactive Reading*

This is intensive, explicit, and focused reading instruction conducted in small groups at the elementary grade level. The elements of reading include phonological awareness, phonics, comprehension, reading fluency, and vocabulary. See www.reading rockets.org/article/28881.

3. *Instructional Conversations and Literature Logs ***

The goal of Instructional Conversations is to help English language learners develop reading comprehension ability along with English language proficiency. Instructional Conversations are small-group discussions. Acting as facilitators, teachers engage English language learners in discussions about stories, key concepts, and related personal experiences, which allows them to appreciate and build on each other's experiences, knowledge, and understanding. Literature Logs require English language learners to write in a log in response to writing prompts or questions related to sections of stories. These responses are then shared in small groups or with a partner. See http://ies .ed.gov/ncee/wwc/reports/english_lang/icll/.

4. *Peer-Assisted Learning Strategies (PALS)*

PALS has been developed for use from preschool through high school. The focus of literacy instruction changes depending on the level of the student, but can include letter-sound correspondence, partner reading, prediction, and so on. It is a structured peer coaching approach in which student pairs work on skills that are causing problems. See http://kc.vanderbilt.edu/pals/faqs/ or

www.cec.sped.org/AM/Template.cfm?Section=Home&TEMPLATE=/CM/Content Display.cfm&CONTENTID=5445.

5. *Read Well*

This program includes systematic instruction in decoding and paired reading with a teacher. Skills are scaffolded to increase confidence and independence. See

http://ies.ed.gov/ncee/wwc/reports/english_lang/read_well/info.asp.

6. *Success for All*

Success for All is a comprehensive reading program that emphasizes systematic phonics, cooperative learning, tutoring for struggling students, family support programs, and other elements. See http://www.successforall.org/_images/pdfs/research_ELL.htm.

7. *Vocabulary Improvement Program for English Language Learners and Their Classmates (VIP) ***

This is targeted vocabulary instruction aligned with weekly reading in upper elementary grades. See http://ies.ed.gov/ncee/wwc/pdf/WWC_VIP_101906.pdf.

* The asterisk denotes programs that were also noted for potentially positive effects in English language development and had no overriding contrary evidence.

Highly Effective Content Programs

According to the National Center for Culturally Responsive Educational Systems (NCCRESt, 2002), effective content resources for teachers have also been identified through the National Association for Bilingual Education (NABE) & IDEA Local Implementation by Local Administrators Partnership (ILIAD) Project. Two examples are:

1. Advancement Via Individual Determination (AVID), designed to teach college-prep English to low-achieving racial and ethnic minorities, embraces strong elements of communal identity, cooperative learning, and reciprocal responsibilities.

2. Math Workshop Program Kamehameha Early Education Program (KEEP) for Native Hawaiian children.

Both of the above programs were found to increase achievement of students when used consistently.

Lives and destinies of people from different cultures, social groups, and backgrounds are often connected by common concerns and dreams. Teachers who take the approach that all students can benefit by helping each other learn to the best of their ability are more likely to develop socially responsible learners. In addition to increased academic performance, students who are part of a cooperative learning community develop stronger feelings of worth, greater satisfaction with school, and more positive relationships across ethnic groups.

Discovering the Cultural Context of Disabilities

Working with diverse students includes being aware and respectful of practices and traditions associated with the culture's primary social or religious beliefs. Both the teacher's world view and the effects of acculturation on a student's family are important factors in honoring culture. Culturally responsive teaching provides opportunity to assess personal knowledge and skills.

Diverse populations may view physical or emotional disabilities in ways that may be very different from your background or experience. Learning disabilities or cognitive disabilities may not be part of the culture. Some common understandings identified by Lynch and Hanson (1999) are noted below. However, to avoid stereotypes it is important to research specific beliefs of the populations with whom you work.

Native American and First Nations People

Disability may be seen by some indigenous populations as the result of either natural or supernatural causes. Spiritual or tribal healers may be asked to conduct ceremonies to restore the balance of nature or ward off evil spirits to protect individuals or families from further harm. Prenatal care may be limited due to certain remote locations of residence. Child-rearing practices are strongly interdependent. Death is seen as part of life's journey.

Asian Populations

Certain Asian populations may see disability as the divine punishment for sins or moral transgressions by parents or ancestors. Throughout pregnancy there are taboos that if not followed are thought to result in disabilities. Generally, severe disabilities, developmental, physical, or sensory impairments, and serious emotional disturbances are viewed with considerable stigma. Lucky charms, spiritual exorcisms, and rituals performed by shamans may be used by families. Family embarrassment or shame, as well as a lack of experience with service providers, may cloak the family's reluctance to seek help. There may be belief that the child will outgrow the condition and be able to fulfill family obligations in order to give the family a good name. Candid discussions of death or serious illness may tempt fate.

Middle Eastern and North African

Arabic people of Islamic tradition typically emphasize good health, personal hygiene, and healthy diets. Some wear amulets for protection or will burn incense to keep the evil eye away from the sick. Muslims are typically a male-dominated society and tend to rely on families, relatives, close friends, or elders for advice, support, and help. They may recommend safe, simple home remedies. In Arab countries, patients are often told only the good news about their disease. In severe cases, the doctors generally tell a family member. Muslims believe recovery from illness has to do with seeking professional treatment and submission to God's will. Death is a destiny decided by God. Some Arabs are reluctant to disclose detailed information about themselves and their families to strangers. Mental illness is considered taboo, and it is rare for such information to be shared with relatives or friends, and it is even more rare to seek professional help.

African

Disability may be considered the work of evil spirits according to some cultural and ethnic populations. Healing rituals may be attempted. Isolating or minimizing involvement through quarantine may be used to avoid contamination of other members of the community when the cause of disability is misunderstood. In some countries, individuals with disabilities are considered sacred.

Latino, Puerto Rican, and Cuban

Some families may believe disability occurs as the result of evil in society. The power of good and evil is often reinforced by Catholic tradition. Orthodox medical practices in tandem with botanicals and herbal remedies or amulets may be used to ensure health or protection from evil spirits. Fatalistic views associated with disability may hinder the use of effective interventions. Extensive grieving and praying accompanies the knowledge that a disability exists.

Refugees and Victims of Torture

Experiences of immigrant populations from countries where violence has been a fact of life must also be considered. Issues of mental health, physical health, stress, fear, anger, withdrawal, and little or no previous academic opportunity may be areas of concern. As refugees, victims of torture, and other immigrant populations resettle in US communities, teachers can learn lessons from health professionals who have been involved in primary care and treatment of significant disabilities. Four challenges are evident according to Meyer (1996). They are:

1. Differentiation. Different ethnic and racial groups have unique health risks.
2. Communication. With or without an interpreter, communication may be difficult as there may be unwillingness to discuss personal matters (such as pregnancy, sexual activity, drug or alcohol use). Having or using a phone may be an obstacle.
3. Respect. Expressing respect rather than impatience for individual beliefs.
4. Mistrust. As a person in authority you may be mistrusted. Prior homeland experiences may have involved leaders who were responsible for horrible crimes.

Even though there may appear to be similarities between cultural groups, do not presume common beliefs. It is important to do the following:

1. Get to know the family as a unit.
2. Determine what meaning the family gives to illness and disability.
3. Ask a cultural broker what the family prefers.

For additional information, excellent references can be found at:

- Cultural Profiles Project (www.settlement.org/cp/english/) is a site that provides in-depth profiles of countries and peoples of the world including social, political, religious, and health customs
- National Council on Disabilities (NCD) (www.ncd.gov) created a helpful guide: *Understanding Disabilities in American Indian and Alaska Native Communities*

- National Immigration Law Center (www.nilc.org) houses a *Guide to Immigrant Eligibility for Federal Programs* including disabilities services that might be needed by newcomers with disabilities
- United States Center for Refugees and Immigrants (USCRI) (http://www .refugees.org/article.aspx?id=2113) has a downloadable brochure with details and pictures designed to introduce the concept of disabilities and educational practices to recent immigrants

In the study of cultures and disability remember:

1. A *stereotype* is an ending point; no attempt is made to learn whether the individual in question fits the statement.

2. A *generalization* is a beginning point; it indicates common trends, but further information is needed to ascertain whether the statement is appropriate to a particular individual (Galanti, 1991).

Cultural backgrounds of children and their families will provide a context for better understanding of beliefs and perspectives. Family histories and views of disability will unfold as trusting relationships develop.

Myths Associated With Teaching Diverse Students With Disabilities

Working with diverse students provides opportunity to review and revise inaccurate thinking. Table 1.1 describes some of the common myths—and realities—associated with ELL instruction.

Misperceptions

The behaviors of ELLs may be misread by teachers as characteristics associated with disabilities (Ortiz, 2004). Consider the following behaviors, which are often reported in referrals when students are suspected of having specific learning disabilities, attention deficit hyperactive disorder, emotional behavioral disorders, traumatic brain injury, and other behavioral or cognitive disorders:

- Disorganized:

  ELLs may not comprehend directions or understand how to organize materials or assignments. The students may not have had previous school experience and may lack efficient work habits.

- Disruptive:

  Behavior such as excessive talking with other ELLs may be the result of frustration or not understanding the expectations.

Table 1.1   Myths and Realities Associated With ELL Instruction

Some Myths:	The Realities:
1. Code switching (using two languages interchangeably when talking) is the sign of a communication disorder.	1. Bilingual students use code switching as a method to clearly express an idea regardless of the language used.
2. Most ELLs are recent immigrants.	2. Data show that 64 percent of ELLs were born in the United States (Flannery, 2009).
3. Learning two languages results in low achievement.	3. Students who learn two languages tend to out-perform monolingual peers.
4. ELLs use native language in class in order to avoid work.	4. ELLs may be attempting to clarify instructions and assignments rather than avoid work.
5. Having an accent indicates a student will need additional service.	5. An accent is an indicator of the point at which a student began to learn a second language.
6. Talking slower to ELLs will improve comprehension.	6. Improved comprehension is the result of using visuals and teaching strategies that are effective with ELLs.
7. Students who do not speak English are found only in large, urban areas.	7. Students who do not speak English are found in many large and small districts throughout the United States.
8. School districts are not obligated to enroll students who are not legal residents of the United States.	8. The federal government mandates that states provide equal public education for undocumented immigrant children (Samway & McKeon, 1999).
9. When ELLs speak their native language in an English-speaking classroom they are likely to be off-task.	9. Such students are about as likely to be off-task as monolingual English speakers (Samway & McKeon, 1999).
10. It is best for ELLs to be pulled out of their regular education classes for English-language instruction.	10. It all depends on the needs of individual students. For some, it may be best that they are not pulled out, whereas pulling others out may best meet the students' educational needs (Samway & McKeon, 1999).

- Distractible:

  In attempting to make sense of the language being used in the classroom, ELLs may attend to many things as they try to comprehend information. They can appear distracted as they look from page to page, teacher to other students, board to book.

- Forgetful:

  Limited comprehension due to lack of English proficiency can cause ELLs to "not get" information rather than "forget."

- Impulsive:

  Hasty work behaviors or lack of following systematic processes may be the result of failure to understand instructions.

- Inattentive:

  ELLs may not know when or what to pay attention to in a classroom due to lack of language comprehension.

- Task Avoidance:

  Slow to begin—ELLs may not know how to start or complete tasks.

  Slow to finish—For some ELLs, time is needed to translate from English to native language and back to English in order to complete a task.

Effective teachers take into consideration the needs of ELLs to avoid confusing various behaviors with an inappropriate diagnosis of a disability.

Analyzing Personal Skills and Competencies

It is important to constantly consider areas to improve professional practice. Professional development enhances a teacher's knowledge and skills. Areas to develop key concepts related to the needs of ELL students with disabilities could include the following:

1. Clarifying the exclusionary clause:

Before students are found to have a specific learning disability, other influences must be considered. The disability must not be the result of hearing, vision, or orthopedic impairment, behavior disorders, or cultural, environmental, or linguistic factors.

2. Defining adequate opportunity to learn:

Determine ways to ascertain the academic history of students. Has the student had access to education, received instruction comparable to peers, had highly qualified teachers?

3. Identifying and implementing meaningful prereferral strategies:

School teams should focus on research-based instructional strategies and data collection to make decisions.

4. Understanding language acquisition as different from communication disorder:

Identify the developmental stages involved in learning a second language. Discuss various characteristics of communication disorders with speech language professionals and levels of academic and social language with ELL teachers.

5. Assessing ELLs:

Be aware of the requirements that must be met before a referral to special education is made. This would also include due process procedures and nondiscriminatory assessment.

6. Including interpreters and other specialists during IEP and Child Study Team meetings:

Formulate a plan for working with specialists knowledgeable of the language and culture of students on IEPs.

Legal Considerations for ELLs

Understanding the cultural and family perspective is one step, but being knowledgeable of the laws that pertain to the rights of ELLs is an additional professional responsibility of the special educator. Federal law IDEA addresses the needs of students whose primary language is not English, including those students who may need information presented through sign language or Braille. For ELLs, the use of trained interpreters will be critical in collecting information from the family, acquiring permission for testing, assessing the learner in the native language, and conducting IEP or other meetings to share results and seek permission for placement.

When working with an interpreter it is important to remember the following:

1. Schedule meetings only after checking with the interpreter first.

2. Brief the interpreter prior to the meeting.

3. Discuss if the interpreter will use simultaneous or delayed interpretation.

4. Provide summaries rather than complex explanations.

5. Avoid jargon. Bring pictures, graphs, and visuals to share.

6. Provide the interpreter with documents to use as references during the meeting.

7. Speak to the parents, not the interpreter, during the meeting.

8. Trust the interpreter. Many special education terms do not exist in other languages. The interpreter may be providing a longer explanation by describing the disability or services in a way the family understands.

9. Trained interpreters are aware of their role in verbatim translation and confidentiality. They relate information and don't give opinions or recommendations.

10. Debrief with the interpreter after the meeting to ensure the family has understood.

Many districts and most states have translated IEPs and other special education documents into a number of different languages. The forms are typically located on the Web sites. The translated Parents' Rights statement, IEP, and other official forms necessary to sign should be readily available at meetings to provide parents with copies of formal documents in their native language.

As schools become more aware of the needs of ELLs with disabilities, administrators and staff will begin to prioritize their professional development needs. Being proactive and positive creates an environment where all students and their families feel like welcome members of a learning community.

Effective Strategies: What Works? Answers to the Activity

Remember the activity earlier in this chapter? Below are the correct answers. How did you do? The top five highly rated strategies in these content disciplines are as follows:

Reading:

1. Preassessment organization strategies

2. Graphic Organizers

3. Cooperative Learning

4. Direct Teaching of Vocabulary

5. Specific Informal Assessments

Math:

1. Curriculum-Based Probes

2. Reciprocal Peer Tutoring

3. Graphic Organizers

4. Explicit Timing

5. Teacher Think-Alouds

Science:

1. Curriculum-Based Probes

2. Graphic Organizers

3. Peer Tutoring

4. Using Short Segments to Teach Vocabulary

5. Using Response Cards During Instruction

Note that graphic organizers are listed as an effective instructional practice across all three content areas. The following common principles are also associated with the practices:

- The practices promote efficient use of time with routines and expectations identified.
- The practices utilize teacher modeling.
- The practices encourage student engagement in the learning process.
- There is documentation of effectiveness.

Pedagogy, in addition to curriculum, must be of high quality since it activates the curriculum. Multiple and varied culturally informed techniques that utilize various teaching and learning styles need to be a part of the teaching repertoire.

SUMMARY

It is important to be aware of the diversity in schools in order to select the instructional strategies that are consistent with student achievement. Students with unique cultural and linguistic backgrounds may come with traditions and academic needs unlike any others you may have experienced. In addition to information obtained from an interpreter, individual research to learn more about social, political, religious, and family customs will help eliminate stereotypes and assist in determining student needs. Professional development can support staff in addressing legal requirements, discovering and using effective pedagogy and curriculum, and dealing with the realities associated with educating an ELL student with disabilities.

SELF-ASSESSMENT AND REFLECTION

After reading Chapter 1, please reflect on your knowledge and skill.

Self-Assessment Items

Respond to the following by answering Yes, Somewhat, or No.

I am able to:

_____ 1. Recognize changing student diversity and demographics;

_____ 2. Describe the impact of diverse populations in special education programming;

_____ 3. Incorporate effective strategies associated with achievement of diverse students with disabilities;

_____ 4. Use the What Works Clearinghouse to identify and provide examples of effective instructional programs;

_____ 5. Compare and contrast the cultural context of disabilities associated with diverse populations;

_____ 6. Address myths associated with teaching diverse students with disabilities;

_____ 7. Analyze personal skills and competencies to increase effectiveness in working with diverse students with disabilities.

Reflection

1. Which of the self-assessment items do you feel fully competent in?

2. Which of the self-assessment items do you feel need some more work, emphasis, or study time?

3. Identify two specific actions that you can take to enrich and strengthen your instructional effectiveness.

2

two—dos—ob

Organizing a Classroom for Instruction

1. Identify methods for organizing classroom space, materials, and time.

2. Identify individuals to serve as contacts and answer questions.

3. Identify practices to organize paperwork and meet timelines.

4. Plan and coordinate schedules for yourself and others.

5. Determine ways to manage and reduce stress.

The instructional continuum varies depending on the needs of students. Today, the least restrictive environment (LRE) more often may be the general education classroom rather than a separate special education site. The evolution of attitudes, legislation, programs, and instruction favors more inclusive practices. Special educators may be assigned a workspace cubicle rather than a special education classroom. Caseloads will include diverse students, as described in Chapter 1, with unique situations, who come and go during the year. This requires organization and flexibility along with professional knowledge and skills.

Effective use of space and resources is a key factor in success for teachers and the students they teach. Organizing the location, instructional materials, paperwork, and time are all components of the educational setting that require preplanning.

In this chapter, a number of proven organizational techniques designed to promote teacher effectiveness and student learning are presented. Special education teachers who work in resource rooms, inclusion classrooms, or variations of either model benefit from being organized. Creativity is often necessary to effectively organize the space designated for teaching. The first step is to be proactive in determining what is needed.

WISDOM OF PRACTICE: MS. DELACATTO—SEE HOW SHE RUNS!

Ms. Delacatto, the new special education teacher, raced through the hallway from the main office where she had been using the phone to have a confidential conversation with a parent. She reached her desk in the team planning room, grabbed a stack of student papers sitting on top of the KeyMath test protocols, and threw them on top of fifteen copies of Gary Paulson's "Hatchet" that were already on the cart. She wheeled the cart through the door at about the same time the bell rang. Hundreds of seventh and eighth graders streamed into the hall from every direction, creating a windstorm that sent Ms. Delacatto's papers flying. Instantly, she remembered she needed a stop watch for Marquis's timed reading. As she whipped the cart around to go back to her cubicle, she collided with Mr. Nelson, the special education lead teacher, who was coming out of the door. The impact caused the novels to scatter everywhere.

Together Mr. Nelson and Ms. Delacatto gathered the books and packed them back on the cart. Ms. Delacatto confessed she really needed help getting organized. She asked Mr. Nelson if he would share some of his ideas with her. They set up a time to meet and Ms. Delacatto identified the goals she wanted to accomplish. After several days of coaching from Mr. Nelson, Ms. Delacatto had established a schedule, grouped student materials and files for easy transportation, and created an accommodating workspace.

IN BRIEF: WHAT DOES THE RESEARCH SAY?

Like Ms. Delacatto, new special education teachers have a lot on their minds. They begin the year in a flurry of activity. With so many things to think about, it is easy to fall behind. Avoidance, procrastination, and poor use of time are counterproductive to effective teaching. Planning and organization, on the other hand, promote success and confidence.

Structural supports are workplace factors that enhance student learning partly because they increase a teacher's job satisfaction. The availability, arrangement, and use of physical space; type, age, and location of materials; and scheduling and time for teaching would be considered structural supports. Administrative support and collegial relationships are also considered structural supports. Lack of support, space, time, and resources are often identified as barriers by new special educators (Billingsley, 2005).

Other researchers have found that skills in managing people, time, resources, curriculum, materials, and space increase effectiveness and job satisfaction (Emmer & Stough, 2001; Otis-Wilborn, Winn, Griffin, & Kilgore, 2005). Whitaker (2001) noted that special education teachers reported feeling overwhelmed with scheduling and organizational responsibilities during their first year of teaching, and rather than appear incompetent they often refrained from asking for help. The Council for Exceptional

Children (2003) supports a minimum of one-year mentorship with such goals as assisting with acculturation to the school climate and reducing stress.

Organization provides more time for teaching and learning. High expectations, standards, and success for teachers and students are reinforced. Organization promotes consistency so students learn how to act. An organized teacher activates trust and supports an environment where there is opportunity to listen, observe, and ask questions.

PROFESSIONAL PRACTICE

New teachers may feel overwhelmed about how to organize a classroom. Other than personal experiences with their own "first days of school" many novice special education teachers have never been required to work in a classroom at the start of a new year. Some first-year teachers mention that lack of "first day" experience as a "hole" in their student teaching. In the excitement of landing the first job of their professional career, the question, "How do I get started?" may never have occurred.

Organizing a Classroom

A special education teacher's role includes scheduling students, selecting materials, establishing workspaces for students and the teacher, completing paperwork, and teaching.

Steps to Get You Started

Visualize the space where you will be working without anything in it. Consider what it will take to become a place for learning. Create a location—whether a resource room, desk, learning center, or inclusive classroom—where you and students can work comfortably and achieve great results. Design an area that is both functional and friendly.

Before starting:

- Review files of students on the caseload;
- Identify student needs;
- Reflect on your teaching style and student expectations.

Next:

- Divide the room into areas where specific tasks are accomplished;
- Generate a master plan for effective use of classroom space for teaching and learning;
- Gather materials to meet student needs and teaching requirements.

Finally:

- Implement the organizational design;
- Assess the success of your plan and "redeploy" materials and furniture as needed.

Organized teachers take the disability and age level of the students into account and then begin to analyze what is needed. A classroom can be designed so flow of traffic and daily activities are compatible.

Defining Spaces

In general, it is helpful to prepare classroom space with the following in mind:

Doors. Hang "Hall Passes" and sign-out sheets on a wall hook near the door. Student lockers or "mailboxes" to drop off and pick up assignments may be located near the entry and exit areas as a reminder to drop off or pick up student work. Some teachers prefer student mailboxes be away from the door to keep from blocking traffic.

Windows. To the extent possible, seat students with their backs to the window.

Shelves. References and student textbooks should be readily accessible on shelves. Writing instruments, paper, and other technology used often during the day can be located around the room in the vicinity of the instruction.

Desks or Tables. Who and what is taught will determine furniture needs and how they will be addressed. Some students work better at a table. This may be true of students with behavior disorders or others who value personal space. Students with autism may need a beanbag option to feel secure. One-piece desks can be too restrictive for some students with physical disabilities.

Quiet Individual Study. Consider a spot for a study carrel or desk away from the hall, computers, and group instruction areas. Have headphones nearby to further decrease distractions.

Small-Group Instruction. Coordinate a table with a shelf nearby to hold books and materials needed for instruction. Keep a full view of the room and avoid having windows behind you. Make sure there is enough space on both the left and right side of your chair to exit should there be an emergency situation you need to address.

Comfortable Reading Spots Near the Leveled Library. Chairs, carpeting, pillows, floor lamps, or a string of lights hung across the ceiling may entice students to hangout and read longer.

Large-Group Instruction. Position the desks to face the board you will use. Have the overhead and screen or the LCD projector and computer close by to facilitate using them. Often, this location is closest to the door, allowing students to move in and out of the room more easily.

Paraeducator's Work Area. Provide a separate desk or table for the paraeducator. Locate your desk at the opposite side of the room to provide adult coverage from two angles.

Student Computers and Other Technology. Locate the outlets first to avoid wires running the length of the room. Identify all technology necessary to work with students.

Teacher Work Area. Arrange the desk to provide some privacy when conducting confidential work. If possible, a teacher-only computer and a phone should be on the desk or wall close to the teacher's desk. A locking cabinet for IEPs and teaching files would be near the desk.

Two "default" floor plans that can be used for a variety of classroom situations are provided. Figure 2.1 provides an example of an elementary room without paraprofessional support. Figure 2.2 might be considered in a secondary class.

Teachers who want to go online to design a to-scale floor plan with furniture for their classroom can download free software such as Classroom Architect from www.4teachers.org. Design options should be considered based on teaching requirements, student needs, and building facilities.

Arranging the Environment

Be a keen observer of how the classroom environment and stimuli impact student behavior. Learn to manage the environment and best meet the needs of students.

| Figure 2.1 | Sample Elementary Special Education Floor Plan |

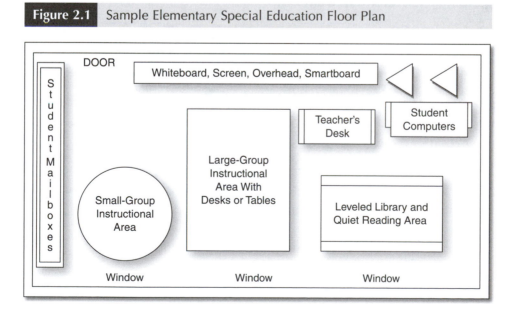

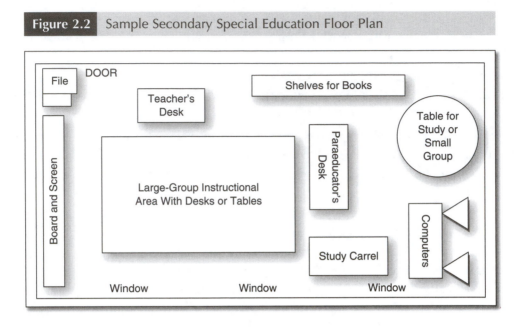

Figure 2.2 Sample Secondary Special Education Floor Plan

Observe whether the "buzz" of a fluorescent lamp affects student behavior. By limiting the number of posters on the wall you may increase student attention. Decide whether student artwork dangling from the ceiling may agitate students. Inadvertently, the arrangement of the physical space and materials in a classroom may serve as a distraction and promote acting out.

Organizing Instructional Materials

Once room arrangement is determined, identify specific furniture, equipment, and instructional materials necessary for teaching. Ask for permission to order the items identified to support student learning. The principal knows the budget, policies, and procedures. It's important to be on time when annual budget requests are made. Itemize and articulate what is required to meet the needs of the students on IEPs.

Anticipating Future Needs of Students

By maintaining an ongoing record of what's been ordered and what is needed, teachers are better prepared to advocate for student and teacher materials. To be proactive consider doing the following:

1. Keep pace with the academic, physical, or behavioral goals of the students with disabilities.

2. Note data on the progress of students. Check trend lines and make predictions of student's anticipated growth to assist in making decisions about future purchases.

3. Have conversations with parents and other professionals involved as members of the IEP team to consider student needs. Be aware of the medical concerns of students and identify issues related to students who might be tactile-defensive.

4. Before spending money, know what is needed and what will be used. Make a list, prioritize the items, and have a plan.

Locating Instructional Materials

When funds are limited or nonexistent, practice the art of "cheapscaping." Many veteran teachers use the following practices to avoid spending an entire paycheck on school materials:

- Recycle and Reuse
  o Check out the district warehouse for "big ticket" items like tables, desks, shelves, and filing cabinets. The warehouse is often a morgue for previously used but still sturdy furniture.
  o Find out if the district has recently reorganized classrooms or buildings. Other materials and equipment may be available.
  o Work with the principal for approval to complete a requisition for the equipment in storage.
  o Request permission for maintenance to pick up and deliver the furniture or remove broken and unwanted items.
  o Retrofit desks, tables, and chairs. Contact the assistive technology staff, an industrial arts teacher, or the district carpenter to redesign the furniture.

- Request Funds From Alternate Sources
  o Ask the special education department chair if there is cash reimbursement for small purchases.
  o Learn how to write grants or request assistance of others trained in the art of securing grants. Often, small funding options, up to $50 to purchase school materials, are available from large corporations such as Target (http://sites.target.com/site/en/company/page.jsp?contentId=WCMP04–031763), Wal-Mart (http://walmartstores.com/), Dollar General (http://www.dollargeneral.com/ServingOthers/Pages/dollar-general-cares-for-you.aspx), or Best Buy (www.best buyinc.com/community_relations/our_programs.htm).
  o Requisition materials necessary to maintain health and safety. This might include purchasing cheap headsets for each child to reduce potential absences associated with head lice infestations, or buying hand sanitizer to help reduce spread of germs.
  o Sign up and have families participate at stores where monetary rebates are returned to schools.
  o Find philanthropic foundations (such as Bill and Melinda Gates) that fund innovative ideas from teachers.

o Check state and federal government agencies that provide grant opportunities. Two common Web sites that list information about grants are www.grantsalert .com and www.grants.gov. If the district has a grant writer, it is important to work with him or her when writing major grants.

o Seek a donation from local organizations such as Lions Club International, Rotary Club, or fraternities and sororities.

o Go to the parent association or the Special Education Advisory Council (SEAC) with a well-written proposal for a specific request.

o Visit local businesses to explain classroom needs to the owner.

o Share ideas with family and friends who may be willing to support the cause.

• Recognize Bargains
  o Locate thrift shops, Goodwill Industries, overstock stores, dollar discount stores, or flea markets.
  o Check garage and estate sales for used furniture and kitchen items.

Maintenance and secretarial staff will be important in helping you locate materials, complying with restrictions (such as using regulation paint without lead), and completing purchase orders.

Developing Routines to Stay Organized

Designate a location for assignments and incoming homework. Teach students to enter the classroom and pick up assignments located in folders at the predetermined spot if it's other than their desk. Use a routine for collecting papers at the end of the day. Hold students responsible for their individual desks, cubbies, and other areas in an effort to keep the room organized. Label locations where items are to be housed.

Organize student equipment and materials by the lesson to be taught. Store items in a plastic bin or box according to content, themes, topics, or months. Color code and label the outside for easy recall. Use the same color for papers filed to coordinate with the lesson.

Working in Inclusive Classrooms

Special education teachers who are coteaching or supporting students in a general education setting will approach organizing their space and day in different ways. The collaborative discussions you initiate will provide a framework for working with students and others. Observing instructional practices, use of materials, and student behaviors in different environments will often prompt the conversations. In inclusive classrooms, talk with the general education coteacher to ensure understanding and agreement. Many of the options discussed in this chapter can be applied creatively in a variety of settings.

Preparing for Itinerant Teaching

Moving from room to room presents a unique set of circumstances. Everything about the day requires staying on schedule and being organized. Instructional materials must be handy for use in a variety of locations. One suggestion is to keep a quart-size plastic bag filled with the following items:

- Sticky notes
- Index cards
- A variety of pencils, pens, and erasers
- Small, blunt scissors
- Paperclips
- A small calendar and tablet
- A deck of cards

- Masking and cellophane tape
- A timer (or stopwatch)
- Highlighting pens or tape
- Overhead pens in a variety of colors
- Rubber bands
- A reliable clock (digital or analog)
- Whiteboard markers or chalk, in a variety of colors, and an eraser

The above items have multiple uses during the day. By keeping the contents portable, they can be quickly retrieved. Other creative ideas will surface throughout the year. Instructional coaches or mentors have a wealth of knowledge to help in selecting materials and preparing instructional spaces. One way to acclimate to teaching and a new classroom is to ask questions.

Asking Questions

New teachers find that asking questions is critical for success. Develop a relationship not only with an assigned mentor but also with other staff who can answer questions and assist with daily issues. School personnel who might serve as contacts to help with new-teacher concerns are identified in Table 2.1.

Don't hesitate to ask questions. If necessary, take the first step to do the following:

1. Introduce yourself and get to know people in the building or district.

2. Find out the best time to talk. Is morning or after school preferred?

3. Determine the best method of communication. Is e-mail or phone more efficient?

4. Establish an appointment for a discussion to get your questions answered.

Time invested in developing relationships will pay dividends in the future. Respect and trust are major components of the communication process. Effective communication includes organizing thoughts, learning to recognize when something is urgent or if the question can wait, and being respectfully assertive.

Organizing Important Information

Novice teachers report they often forget important information as they deal with a crisis, teach, or hold multiple conversations. Days may pass and, without documenting items, information is forgotten. Related service providers are great resources for information on how to stay organized, manage a tight schedule, and follow through with paperwork.

Table 2.1   School Contacts: Duties and Concerns

Contact Person	Description of Duties	Possible Concerns
Adaptive Physical Education Teacher	Physical education teacher who has knowledge and skill in working with students with cognitive, physical, social, and behavioral disabilities.	What are suggestions for involving all students in games at recess?
Assistive Technology Coordinator	Person who designs, services, or provides assistive technology or training on how to use it.	What is assistive technology?
Content or Discipline Area Coaches	Teachers trained to assist in the implementation of specific content instruction.	Where are the best teachers who can be observed?
Counselor • Elementary • Secondary	Facilitates acceptance of self and others. Works with students to ensure that graduation and goals for future are met.	How do I prepare classes for including students with disabilities? How many credit hours have been earned toward graduation?
Department Chair	A tenured teacher designated to communicate information to and from the principal and teachers.	How do we schedule classes for students?
District Curriculum Specialist	A person with understanding and expertise in content standards (such as math, language arts, health, and so on) and alignment with local curriculum.	Where is the list of standards for each grade level?
English Language Learner Specialist	Individual trained to work with non-native speakers of English.	What is the expectation for using academic language by grade level?
Instructional Technology	Person in charge of the computer software and hardware.	How do I access the electronic IEP?

Contact Person	Description of Duties	Possible Concerns
Mobility Specialist	Person who trains individuals to orient themselves in and outside of a building and in the community.	When do we involve the student in more community experiences?
Nurse	Medical professional assigned to schools.	Who dispenses medicine when the nurse is gone?
Occupational Therapist	Professional who works with fine motor skills.	Are there exercises that assist with handwriting?
Physical Therapist	Professional who designs plans for increasing large motor skills.	What is the best way to lift a student from the wheel chair?
Police Liaison Officer	Person who assists with controlling student behavior.	How do I reach you in an emergency?
School Psychologist	Individual qualified to conduct and interpret psychological assessments.	How do we inform parents what the testing results mean?
Social Worker	Professional trained to deal with mental health and social welfare issues.	What are the local services for families in conflict?
Special Education Director	Administrator who has oversight of the compliance with academic and legal requirements of students on IEPs.	What do I do now that the caseload exceeds the legal limits in our state?
Team Lead	Person who facilitates team meetings or coordinates resources to support special educators.	Who sends out the notice of meetings?
Union Representative	Individual who communicates contract concerns for teachers.	I've been asked to substitute during my prep period. What does that mean?
Work Coordinator or Transition Specialist	Person who trains students for a job in the community.	Where do we find employers?

Documenting Information

Get a Lesson Plan Book. Many districts provide these to teachers at the beginning of the year. Besides documenting what objectives and lessons you are teaching, jot notes to help you recall essential information from conversations.

Create Charts. Completed daily (Table 2.2) or weekly (Table 2.3), organization charts are tools for recording important information. Use neon colored, 8½-by-11-inch paper so it stands out. Attach the chart to a clipboard, insert it in the planning book, or place in an "in-basket" or binder on your desk, and use it!

Table 2.2 Sample Daily Organization Chart

Who	What	When	Why	Where	How
1. Teacher _____	Observe Sarah M.	8:00–8:20 a.m.	Behavior check.	Room 212, English	
2. Para	Listen to Ben F. read	8:20–8:30	Note errors plus length of time	SPED room	Frequency Chart 100-word passage (IRI)

Table 2.3 Sample Weekly Organization Chart

Date	Found Out	Need to Know	Must Do
Monday Feb. 6	Sam C.—asthma attack	Medication changed?	Call parent
Tuesday Feb.7	Trent L.P.—needs 3 year re-evaluation Jedica B.—moving Fri.	Deadline? Identify assessments needed WHERE!!!!	Notify assessment team members Are forms updated?
Wednesday Feb. 8	B. Two Hawks = New 2nd grader	Where's the IEP?	Ask secretary to call previous school!
Thursday Feb. 9	Jen W. skipped math	Principal did what?	Schedule manifestation determination for Tues.
Friday Feb. 10		Holiday!	

Charts provide documentation of what has been or needs to be done. Other ideas include the following:

Invest in a digital voice recorder. These typically cost under $40. The device is about the size of a cell phone and can be kept in a pocket. Hallway conversations or information from a phone call can be quickly noted, listened to later, and transferred into the student's file or electronic log. Determine a specific time of the day when data and conversations will be documented in the contact log.

Use a Personal Data Assistant (PDA). These are handy to enter a quick text message and download it to the computer later. Keep the device in a pocket. A fanny pack, plastic sleeve in three-ring binder, a large manila envelope attached to a clip board, or a desk drawer have all been used effectively as failsafe PDA storage locations. Individuals prone to forgetting or setting things down and walking away might opt for another communication device.

Purchase a clipboard. It is a low tech and inexpensive multipurpose tool for keeping data, messages, and notes. Buy a sturdy clipboard, one that holds 8½-by-11-inch paper, not the legal size. Use a permanent marker to write your name on it. Attach an 8-inch piece of string to secure a pen or pencil to the clipboard. Record data during classroom observations, jot recommendations at a team meeting, or, if you are using a phone in another room, you can take notes of the conversation. This organizational tool promotes a process that keeps all important reminders clipped to the board until there is time to deal with each issue in a methodical and logical sequence.

Creating a Message System

Whether using a handmade chart or technology, the key is to follow a routine.

Develop a plan to take and keep messages. Most but not all classrooms have a phone with a whiteboard, chalkboard, or corkboard hung near the phone. If the room doesn't have a phone or message board, ask for one. Messages written on scraps of paper get lost in the shuffle of paper on top of a desk. Too often, key pieces of information get lost, data is overlooked, or phone numbers get misplaced and time gets wasted. A tablet, clipboard, or three-ring binder with a pencil attached can be hung on a hook near the phone. Small magnetic baskets can be attached to white boards to hold extra pens, markers, or sticky notes for messages.

Organize messages. Choose a practice that best fits your situation. You may have a variety of sticky notes or colored paper available for messages. Select one color such as bright green for urgent, high-priority student items. Use yellow for personal reminders or messages. Use blue for teaching or instructional plans. Mark an office tray for messages, set it on your desk, and use it as an in-box for all messages. Be consistent and teach others who work with you to use the same routine.

Tech-ready teachers use the computer as an indispensable organizational tool. Electronic files for student data, lesson plans, and spreadsheets for organizing the calendar support effective teaching and workload duties.

Organizing Schedules for Yourself and Others

Special education teachers not only have students to manage, but often there are paraeducators in the classroom working with students on IEPs.

Working With Paraeducators

Educational or instructional assistant, teacher's aid, paraeducator, or paraprofessional are different names districts use for the adult hired as a support person. Adults who have been assigned to work with students on IEPs in the special or general education classroom will need consistent direction and support. Communicating daily responsibilities and student information between teacher and paraeducator can be done in several effective ways.

One suggestion is to plot the students' daily schedules on a whiteboard. Write the name of the paraeducator on a sticky note and stick it to the name of the student or duty that needs attention. The sticky note is moved as the day progresses and students' needs are identified.

Another idea is to place a three-ring binder in a central location, such as the teacher's desk, which is designated for adults in the room and is off limits to students. In this notebook, each teacher and paraeducator writes daily comments related to student activities, success, or concerns. A chart similar to Table 2.4 can be used to document who is doing what, when, and where. As a team, set a time to debrief about events that are recorded. That collaboration time may only be five minutes, but plan to communicate daily.

The paraeducator's contract will determine what hours and responsibilities are involved.

- Be aware of what the paraeducator can or cannot do.
- Identify training he or she needs to effectively work with students.
- Teach the paraeducator specific academic, behavioral, or documentation strategies to be used with the student.
- Establish a written communication procedure (see Table 2.4).
- Incorporate good suggestions made by the paraeducator.
- Train yourself to give feedback that is specific.
- Know who is responsible for the formal evaluation process of the paraeducator.

Table 2.4	Sample Paraeducator-Teacher Communication Chart

	Paraeducator's Name Meg	Teacher Comments	Paraeducator Comments
Monday Date: Dec. 12	Student(s): Xiong Measurable Objective: 80% correct on written vocabulary Location of Work: SPED room Materials Needed: Fourth-grade science book	Read aloud Ch. 2 vocab test. (No excuses from him!)	He got 8/10!
Tuesday Date: Dec. 13	Student(s): Tina Measurable Objective: Create graphic organizer of evaporation cycle Location of Work: Fourth-grade class Materials Needed: Science book	Tina is to describe the water cycle, then create a GO.	She was creative. (Volunteered to explain the cycle in class.)

Scheduling Students

Looking at the big picture is necessary. It may seem very complex at the beginning of a year. Sometimes it takes a week or longer to refine student and teacher schedules. The following items will help this process run more smoothly:

- Start by identifying student needs as designated in the IEP.
- Consider the settings where instruction will be provided.
- Look at the availability of professionals who provide related services.
- Determine what times are designated for lunch or specials.
- Find out if there are firm, nonnegotiable times scheduled during the day or week.
- Plot all of these on a whiteboard or a spreadsheet.
- Strategize unique ways to group students or use the paraeducator.
- Coordinate a daily schedule by building in time to assess, observe, and write reports.
- Compromise with others when necessary.

Scheduling may be one of the times to consult a mentor or the principal for assistance.

Maintaining Student Paperwork

A student's cumulative student file contains all information associated with each grade level. This includes annual grades along with teacher comments, data related to retention or promotion, standardized test scores, pictures, medical history, and a record of disciplinary actions, absences, and times tardy to class. A cumulative file is kept in the principal's office and is sent, upon request, to a new school when the student moves.

The IEP file holds the current and previous IEPs for the student. Along with that, each of the assessment protocols establishing continuing need for special education and summary reports of the annual meetings or any other meeting held as part of the student's education are kept in the IEP file. Each time the parent is contacted, a record of the conversation, including time and date, is noted in the IEP file. In most cases, IEPs are kept in the special education room in a locked cabinet.

IEPs and personally identifiable student information are protected by the Family Educational Rights and Privacy Act (FERPA) and similar legislation that restricts who has access. Other confidential information is included in student files so individuals reviewing the IEP or cumulative folders are required to sign and date as well as briefly identify their purpose for reviewing the documents. As a special education teacher it is imperative to have a desk or file cabinet that can be locked. The teacher's computer should have limited or no student access.

Working files are those related to daily progress on goals and objectives and include documentation charts and other comments about instruction. Review each of the students' IEPs for details. Organize information for each student on your caseload into a three-ring binder, folder, or electronic file. Gather the following information:

1. *Student Data.* Include a home address and working phone number to reach a family member or adult guardian. A cell phone is often the best number to call.

2. *Student Identification Number.* This avoids mistakes associated with student names that are similar.

3. *Emergency Contact Information.* Be aware if both parents are to be contacted or if there are legally binding family circumstances such as restraining orders.

4. *Medical Needs.* Include doctors, clinics, phone numbers, and prescriptions.

5. *Daily and Weekly Schedule.* Identify teachers and room locations.

6. *Instructional Information.* Include courses, credits, and requirements.

7. *Behavioral Information.* Note what works and what doesn't.

8. *Documentation Charts.* Select and use a progress monitoring system.

9. *Dates for Next Annual IEP and Three-Year Reevaluation.* Highlight these.

10. *Other Pertinent Information.* This might include primary language, assistive technology needs, or transition services.

11. *Related Services.* Note what is required, the service provider, and the number of minutes, as well as the location where the service is being provided in compliance with the Federal Setting requirements.

12. *Assignments.* Collect exemplary papers and those that demonstrate successes and areas where work may be needed.

Meeting Due-Process Timelines

Compliance dates and timelines are critical management issues. Note the following items:

1. For each student on the caseload, write the annual IEP or three-year reevaluation date on the calendar. This date is a deadline by when all assessments must be given and scored, information gathered, a team meeting held, and a new IEP completed.

2. Depending on procedural guidelines established by the special education administrator in the district, request parental permission for the reevaluation 30 to 60 days before the IEP due date.

3. Allow ten days for the Notice of the IEP Meeting to go to parents, teachers, and other professionals who will be involved.

Using Time Effectively

New special education teachers often seek guidance for effective use of time. It is common for assessments, IEPs, and lesson planning to take more time at the beginning of your career. Make a list of what must be done in a day or week. Prioritizing what to do first, second, and so on provides a methodical process to get through one day at a time. Physically checking items off the list creates a visual sense of accomplishment.

Preparing for Daily and Weekly Tasks

Arrive at school at least fifteen minutes before the contract time specifies. Review the daily schedule. Make sure materials needed for the lesson and meetings are available. Preparations completed the night or weekend before ensure latitude when an unforeseen situation occurs. Each Friday, review the next week's calendar to see what assessments are scheduled, which reports are due, and what meetings are planned. Review the notes that you have written during the day. Log all contacts and check e-mails and voice messages daily.

Plotting a Global Vision of the Year

At the beginning of the school year, get a calendar and mark events. Use the same calendar all year, adding meeting dates and times as they occur. Don't forget to identify the following events:

- Professional development days,
- Civic or school holidays,
- Required staff or department meetings,
- Midterm or end of semester,
- "Child Find" date,
- IEP and ESR due dates,
- Parent-teacher conferences,
- Report card and progress monitoring due dates,
- Predetermined emergency drills,
- Field trips that special education students take in your class and other disciplines.

Certain times of the year tend to be more anxiety producing for teachers. For new teachers, the year starts with a steep learning curve that increases rapidly between October and December. January and February often provide a plateau for teaching before giving standardized tests. Referrals, assessments, IEP meetings, transition, and exit reports explode between March and May. The level of intensity and activity is maintained until it ends abruptly in June. Although events vary by district and individual schedules, Table 2.5 (see opposite) lists several sample monthly activities.

Knowing the schedule of events and planning ahead can relieve anxiety about the work you need to accomplish. In addition, it is important to balance a career with other activities in your life.

Staying Organized and Managing Stress

One of the gifts you can give yourself during the early years of teaching is to keep the job in perspective. Build good habits and work on eliminating risky behaviors. Ideas for reducing stress and staying healthy come from many sources including health insurance companies, professional organizations, doctors, family and friends. Some suggestions include the following:

1. Organize your personal life. Make lists.

2. Eat healthy. Plan and shop for meals weekly.

3. Practice preventive health care. Get a flu shot. Note other medical issues that need to be resolved.

4. Decide what to wear before you go to bed at night.

5. Spend time with friends.

6. Exercise and look for new ways to be active.

7. Listen to music or sing out loud.

8. Leave work and problems at school.

Table 2.5	Sample Monthly Guide to Job Responsibilities

Month	Activity
August	Settle into a new job and location. Meet other staff. Locate rooms and materials.
September	Receive and review files of students on the caseload. Coordinate teaching responsibilities. Collaborate with others to schedule related services.
October	Attend inservices and provide on-site training for teachers. Prepare for a formal observation by the principal. Send out grades and progress reports.
November	Hold parent-teacher conferences. Get initial referrals after the eight weeks of interventions. Review student data on reading and math. Initiate all curriculum-based measurements as required.
December	Child Count data is due. All IEPs must be in compliance. Meet regularly with coteaching, prereferral, content, or department teams. Address student behaviors and hold manifestation determinations. Plan for holiday events.
January	Conduct on-going observations, formal, and informal evaluations. Write assessment reports. Coordinate IEP meetings. Attend all required professional development sessions.
February	Plan for substitute teachers. Prepare for flu season, absences, and make-up work. Provide on-going training for paraprofessionals. Send out grades and progress reports.
March	Notice of contract renewals is given. Consider transition plans.
April	Proctor standardized tests. Hold IEP meetings.
May	Complete end of year assessments and reports.

9. Determine if the situation is one you have no control over.

10. Keep smiling.

Staying socially, emotionally, and physically healthy can also be a factor in changing your professional perspective and performance to be more positive and productive.

SUMMARY

Effective use of time, space, and resources are key factors in success for teachers and the students they teach. Organizing the location, instructional materials, paperwork, and time are ingredients in the educational setting new special educators must juggle. Being proactive, setting schedules, and coordinating responsibilities as the year begins are steps in managing work. In addition, having interests and outlets unrelated to professional responsibilities can help reduce stress.

SELF-ASSESSMENT AND REFLECTION

After reading Chapter 2, please reflect on your knowledge and skill.

Self-Assessment Items

Respond to the following by answering Yes, Somewhat, or No.

I am able to:

_____ 1. Identify methods for organizing classroom space, materials, and time;

_____ 2. Identify individuals to serve as contacts and answer questions;

_____ 3. Identify practices to organize paperwork and meet timelines;

_____ 4. Plan and coordinate schedules for myself and paraeducators;

_____ 5. Determine ways to manage and reduce stress.

Reflection

1. Which of the self-assessment items do you feel fully competent in?

2. Which of the self-assessment items do you feel needs more work, emphasis, or study time?

3. Identify two specific actions you can do to enrich and strengthen your instructional effectiveness.

3

three—tres—peb

Managing Student Behavior

OBJECTIVES

1. Analyze classroom management needs.

2. Discuss the three levels used to manage student behaviors.

3. Identify effective practices for preventing inappropriate student behaviors

4. Identify practices that increase positive student behaviors.

5. Determine effective interventions when inappropriate student behavior occurs.

6. Identify skills and behaviors students need to successfully prepare for the future.

7. Discuss legal rights and professional ethics that guide work with students.

Special education teachers consider how to design educational experiences that will benefit a student. The student's disability frames his or her academic need and placement. Similar to all classrooms, students in special education classes have very diverse backgrounds and experiences. Caseloads consist of students who have parents or other adults who may or may not believe in them and their potential. Students on IEPs may have many, few, or no friends. On the outside, some students with disabilities appear no different than thousands of students attending classes every day. Others, however, will come kicking and screaming.

Some schools have implemented positive behavioral supports throughout the building to help reduce classroom management issues and provide more time for student achievement. When working with students who are on IEPs for behavior concerns, specific plans for managing individual student behavior will be necessary. This chapter introduces three levels of managing student behavior—prevention, intervention (ranging from least to most intrusive), and maintenance—to create the classroom equilibrium needed for teaching and learning. Replacing inappropriate behaviors with skills known to support future success will assist in planning IEPs. Professional standards of conduct used to guide decisions in managing student behavior are also discussed.

WISDOM OF PRACTICE:
MR. DOWNING—THE PRINCIPAL IS WATCHING!

Principal Minema walked into the special education room. It was a huge classroom, approximately one-eighth the size of a gymnasium. That was how the eight students were treating it—like a gym. The high ceilings with fluorescent lighting had an array of spit wads dangling from the worn tiles. The teacher, Mr. Downing, and two paraprofessionals, Lauren and Bill, looked like they were engaged in a basketball game.

The adults moved around the room locked in one-on-one defense with students in an effort to establish control. Intermittently, one of the students on the side would make a verbally abusive comment and dart to another area of the room. The distraction would disengage Mr. Downing from one potentially explosive student and create opportunity for another student to get into the "game" after refueling. It was clear Mr. Downing's reserve of patience was exhausted.

Mrs. Minema saw a classroom that was in chaos. Mr. Downing lacked a plan. Students were in charge. The misuse of academic time, the inconsistency of teamwork, and the repeated threats without follow-through provided evidence that neither teaching nor classroom management were intact.

Fortunately for Mr. Downing, Mrs. Minema blew the whistle. She was able to support him in restoring order. Later that day, they met to identify areas where professional development and coaching would assist him in building his repertoire of effective classroom management and instructional strategies.

IN BRIEF: WHAT DOES THE RESEARCH SAY?

One reason novice teachers give for leaving the profession is that they have been unprepared or underprepared to effectively manage student behaviors (Oliver & Reschley, 2007). Once on the job, their experiences leave them physically and emotionally drained (Berliner, 1986; Espin & Yell, 1994). New teachers often report that they receive little or no support from principals and other administrators (Baker, 2005; US Department of Education, Office of Special Education Programs, 2002).

Student behavior is known to impact teaching behavior in many ways. There is overwhelming evidence that teacher job satisfaction and retention are linked to managing student behavior (Baker, 2005; Ingersoll & Smith, 2003). More and better instruction occurs in a well-managed classroom. In addition, there is a strong connection between student achievement and teacher efficacy (Emmer & Stough, 2001). Inability of teachers to effectively manage a class continues the cycle of low achievement for at-risk and special needs students (Donovan & Cross, 2002).

A well-disciplined academic and social environment and a school culture with practices that support high standards and student achievement are known to be effective for increasing achievement (Elliot, 2007). Managing student behavior is a schoolwide and an individual teacher responsibility (Scott, Liaupsin, Nelson, & McIntyre, 2005). When student behavior gets in the way of academics or safety the behavior must be addressed.

PROFESSIONAL PRACTICE

Working with students who have severe behaviors or cognitive or physical disabilities may test a teacher's limits. On a given day there will be:

- Expletives or violent outbursts from students,
- Concerns about maintaining the health and safety of the class,
- Paperwork to complete according to timelines,
- Difficult meetings with parents, and
- Confidential student information to handle with sensitivity.

Doing the Right Thing: Professional Ethics

Sometimes competing requirements and obligations cause stress. In order to ensure quality in educational practice as well as to protect teachers and students, professional organizations implement ethics and standards of conduct. A code of ethics ensures standards of behavior are applied across the profession.

The CEC Code of Ethics for Educators of Persons with Exceptionalities, located at www.cec.sped.org, identifies special education teachers' responsibilities. It includes agreeing to

- Uphold the rights of students with disabilities;
- Provide education that develops the student's potential and quality of life;
- Demonstrate and promote honesty, integrity, and competence in practice;
- Increase knowledge and use research-based practice;
- Engage in professional activities designed to enhance work with students, families, and other professionals;
- Exhibit decision making that is objective and professional.

The National Education Association (NEA) has a Code of Ethics of the Education Profession, which applies to all teachers and can be found at www.nea.org. NEA's Code of Ethics includes a section titled "Commitment to the Student." When dealing with student behavior, all teachers are obliged to:

- Protect students' health and safety,
- Avoid harmful learning situations,

- Refrain from intentionally embarrassing or discrediting students or placing students in situations where they may be vulnerable;
- Avoid discriminatory practices, and
- Maintain privacy of student information.

Each state has professional licensure expectations that can be obtained from individual Department of Education Web sites and are included with an official teaching license. As part of the licensure process, teachers agree to follow and uphold the ethics of the profession. These standards are helpful to remember when dealing with difficult behaviors.

Managing student behavior requires a consistent approach. Highly qualified special education teachers support students with disabilities in managing their behaviors. Well-defined practices can be used to prevent or reduce the likelihood of misbehavior, intervene when inappropriate behaviors occur, and maintain appropriate student behaviors. The climate of the whole school can be useful in addressing the daily behaviors of students with disabilities.

Schoolwide Positive Behavioral Interventions and Supports

Schools that are successful in establishing an academic setting where learning is valued and student achievement is evident have generally made managing behaviors a building-wide responsibility. Five components of such an approach include the following:

1. A commitment to address student behaviors with consistency across classes and common spaces.

2. A visible principal who is involved as a member of the staff and invested in the process and outcome.

3. Student issues that are discussed, documented, and dealt with as a team.

4. Clearly identified roles and responsibilities of a Teacher Assistance Team (TAT).

5. Regular team meetings to discuss documentation as part of a prereferral process.

These practices are often being developed as schoolwide positive behavioral support (SWPBS) systems or positive behavioral supports (PBS). The intentional focus on a systematic process prior to special education referral promotes a number of factors:

1. Both the teacher and the student are supported.

2. Data related to the behavior is collected.

3. Schools see an increase in positive behaviors.

4. There is less over-representation or misplacement of diverse students in special education.

Holding all students to the same high expectations behaviorally as well as academically means expectations will need to be made clear and taught to students. Some schools target specific skills at various grade levels. Data collected on recurring and severe infractions guide decisions. Teacher leadership and curriculum discussions, along with administrative support, are necessary to implement positive behavioral interventions and support (PBIS).

A number of effective, researched-based curricula exist to assist in teaching positive behaviors. Examples of programs school districts use are: Adolescent Curriculum for Communication and Effective Social Skills (ACCESS) by Walker, Todis, Holmes, and Horton (1988); ASSET: A Social Skills Program for Adolescents by Sheldon-Wildgen, Sherman, Schumaker, and Hazel, (1981); CHAMPS: A Proactive and Positive Approach to Classroom Management developed by Randy Sprick in conjunction with Safe and Civil Schools (1998); the Boys Town Education Model (BTEM) initiated in 1970 and since revised; and Goldstein and McGinnis's Skillstreaming model (1997). These and other programs are selected to teach specific skills that support all learners.

Whether or not a school has elected to implement PBS, it is important for special education teachers to be prepared to manage difficult student behaviors. There are generally three levels involved in managing student behavior:

1. Prevention

2. Intervention

3. Maintenance

The levels are successively more premeditated and deliberate. In each level there are methods of managing behavior that will work well with some students and not others.

Level One: Preventing Student Misbehaviors

Teachers who manage student behaviors effectively are able to identify and use a repertoire of options. The first step is to prevent as many inappropriate behaviors from occurring as possible. There are a number of ways to do this.

Analyze the Situation

It is important to analyze each instructional situation. The type of disability and setting will call for unique and individualized approaches. Think through various activities that occur in the classroom. Even the simplest activity can generate misbehavior. Jot down those areas most problematic in a particular location, at a specific time, or with certain students. Identify and clarify the expectations that are most important for managing student behavior in the class.

It can be helpful to have an academic coach or mentor observe and document behaviors while you are working with students.

Establish Routines, Procedures, and Rituals

Managing student behavior involves setting up positive guidelines and expectations that establish order in the classroom. A routine is something the students do automatically. The procedure is what the teacher wants done. It is important to model and have students practice these more than once. Two examples are as follows:

1. Routine: Get out a book to read or complete other work.

   Procedure: Sit quietly in the desk.

2. Routine: Write your name and time on the board.

   Procedure: Take a bathroom break only when necessary.

Special education teachers often display posters with routines identified. Visuals of what a behavior looks like, such as a "calm body," serve as reminders of the expectations.

Rituals are different than routines. Rituals can be implemented as transitions or methods of recognizing accomplishments. Examples include:

- playing music in the room as students enter the classroom,
- signaling academic transitions between subjects by using an African rain stick, or
- using "exit" passes (such as a handshake or high-five) at the end of a day to ensure students leave with an affirmation.

Teaching and promoting consistent routines and rituals eliminates student confusion and helps prevent misbehavior. Routines and rituals support student independence and reinforce the likelihood that students will engage in self-management skills.

Build Relationships With Students

Experienced teachers know that positive relationships with students are a fundamental deterrent to misbehavior. It may take some time to build trust, but get to know a student as an individual. Show interest and engage the student in conversation. Incorporate the following ideas:

1. Listen intently and empathetically, without interruption or judgment.

2. Be curious about the student's activities. Ask questions that promote communication.

3. When appropriate, share experiences or hobbies. Students like to know a teacher is "real."

4. Be genuine and honest.

5. Look for cultural influences that impact the student's behavior. Seek out background knowledge and family history of the student.

A relationship of trust between a teacher and student requires not only the ability to be open but also the confidence to say "No."

Establish Boundaries

Clear boundaries promote the student-teacher relationship and support classroom management. Teach limits by modeling respect and self-restraint. Provide guidance for students. Be consistent with your responses to classroom rules.

The Broken Record

The "broken record" uses a precise statement that explains what the expectation is and the consequence of not following through. An example is: "I know you are a social person and really want to talk to your friends now, but this is the time devoted to writing in the journal. You need to go to your desk and write. If you do not write, you do not earn points."

The student has been affirmed, given the direction, and knows the consequence when the teacher request is ignored. Separate out emotion and stay with the facts. Decide if you will repeat the "broken record" response two or more times, but follow through with the consequence.

Develop a Sense of Humor

A sense of humor goes a long way when developing a relationship with students. Teachers who are able to laugh at themselves and their mistakes may seem more approachable to students. Humorous statements can also be used to diffuse potentially explosive situations. A witty response timed just right may catch a student off guard and lower the level of aggression.

Humor is powerful when used carefully, however, there are caveats:

- A statement is not funny if it is said at the expense of another person.
- Avoid sarcasm. Sarcasm is a cutting remark that is generally used to ridicule another person and in so doing, it creates a victim.

Implement Effective Instruction

A primary factor in preventing inappropriate student behavior is effective instruction. What is taught and how it is taught involves knowledge and skill. Instruction is based on the student's age and content standards. The IEP goals serve as an annual benchmark to assist in documenting progress. When preparing a lesson, know the students' developmental and instructional levels. Planning well increases opportunities to learn and reduces opportunities for students to misbehave. Consider the following:

1. Give clear directions. a) Read directions out loud to yourself or someone else; b) Avoid too many steps and keep them simple; c) Eliminate using too many pronouns.

2. Pace lessons. Assign a realistic amount of time for each activity. Keep the lesson moving.

3. Challenge all students. Set and hold high expectations.

4. Increase interest. Begin with a mystery, problem to solve, or puzzle.

5. Ask questions that cause students to think, such as, "I wonder what would happen if . . . ?"

6. Provide choice. Differentiate the method of instruction, student response, materials, and assessment.

7. Ensure relevance. Connect the lesson to a situation that students recognize.

Subsequent chapters in this book focus on effective instruction, designing and using active student learning, and using graphic organizers strategically in the classroom. Effective teachers are proactive in preventing misbehaviors when they implement effective instructional strategies. Thoughtfully planned instruction can be coordinated with periodic review of the setting where a student is placed.

Conduct an Ecological Inventory

When working with students who are in inclusive classrooms, an ecological inventory or environmental scan can provide initial and continuing information for making good academic decisions about the match between the teacher, other students, what is taught, how it is taught, and where it is taught. Systematically making a list and discussing students' behavioral and academic strengths and needs can provide insight needed by both the special and general education teacher. The same type of inventory can be conducted in resource or self-contained special education classrooms. Appropriate placements and physical arrangements help prevent inappropriate behavior. One example of an ecological inventory is given in Table 3.1.

Some students' behaviors intensify and require another level of management from proactive prevention to active intervention.

Level Two: Intervening When Misbehavior Occurs

New special education teachers grapple with ways to develop authority. Interventions that are too harsh or inconsistent may be the first sign there is trouble in

Table 3.1 Ecological Inventory

Student: _____

Classroom/Subject: _____

Completed by: _____

Date: _____

Check if there is a match for the student. Note specific needs to be addressed.

	Match	Student Needs	Teacher Needs
1. Room Arrangement: Supports learning and is safe and comfortable			
2. Technology: UDL is incorporated and used to support learning			
3. Organization of Materials: Procedures are in place and all students are accountable			
4. Curriculum and Resources: Student has access to a variety of materials			
5. Instructional Strategies: Learning is differentiated			
6. Classroom Environment: Expectations are clear and distractions are limited			
7. Student Engagement: Students are involved in goal setting and can describe learning			
8. Assessment: Formative, specific, and timely feedback			

(Continued)

	Match	Student Needs	Teacher Needs
Table 3.1 (Continued)			
9. Evaluations: Unbiased, valid and reliable			
10. Homework Expectations: Clear directions; opportunity for questions is provided			
11. Teacher and Other Adults: Demonstrate inclusivity, smile, act professional			
12. Peers: Students look happy, and are respectful of diversity			

managing student behaviors. At level two, the interventions become more focused on reducing or eliminating inappropriate behaviors. Interventions begin with the least amount of intrusion and move up the ladder of intensity to those that are more intrusive.

Behavior that is harmful to self or others is always considered a priority in order to ensure safety. Behaviors identified on IEPs may include poor social skills, antagonism toward authority, or self-deprecating statements. Behavioral goals, like academic goals, are observable, methodically taught, and documented with data.

Managing behaviors involves discipline rather than punishment. As a special education teacher, it will be important to teach appropriate skills to replace those that are deficient. Discipline is derived from a Latin term that when translated means "to guide" or "teach." On the other hand, punishment is punitive and generally limits or reduces the possibility of students internalizing the intended lesson.

Not every behavior is able to be addressed at once. Separate annoying behaviors from "out of control" behaviors. Experienced teachers suggest new special educators "pick their battles." The key is to be explicit with what behavior is allowed and what the consequences are. Interventions should be designed to match the severity of the behavior. Intervention strategies are implemented on a continuum from least to most intrusive.

Naturally Occurring Interventions

Strategies that are portable and easy to apply in a variety of situations or locations would be at the least intrusive end of the continuum. They are often for behaviors identified as annoying but not major threats. Naturally occurring interventions in a well-managed classroom would include the following:

- The "teacher look": A stern and strategically timed glance.
- Proximity control: Standing near a student or continuously moving around the room.
- Physical gesture: The teacher taps or places a hand on the student's desk or gently touches the student's shoulder.
- Verbal prompt, cue, or reminder: "It's important to listen now."
- Auditory prompt: Turn on music, ring a bell, or clap to redirect attention.
- Visual prompt, cue, or reminder: Holding up a hand to signal a stop or turn off the lights momentarily.
- Peer pressure or praise: "I see Quito is sitting quietly and ready to begin the test."
- Precorrection activities: Model and practice expectations in order to limit the occurrence of inappropriate behavior.

Planned Interventions

Inappropriate behaviors that occur regularly and have propensity to get out of control require a greater level of intervention. Management tools can be designed to work effectively in a classwide environment or as a student-specific intervention. Examples of planned interventions are as follows:

Teach Problem-Solving. Teach and use a problem-solving model that requires the student to be involved in the process. One example is SODAS (Rosa, 1973), where students are taught to name the problem, brainstorm solutions, and implement an option using the following steps:

S = Situation: The specific problem is defined.

O = Options: Three options to remedy the situation are identified.

D = Disadvantages: For each option, list two or three disadvantages.

A = Advantages: For each option, brainstorm two or three advantages.

S = Solution: Select the best option, implement, and schedule a time to discuss results.

Implement a Contract. Contracts specifically identify the student's problem behavior. The key is to list a positive behavior as a measurable goal. Include a specified period of time. Identify student and teacher responsibilities necessary to achieve the goal. Both the student and teacher are involved in negotiating the terms and each signs the contract. Below is one example of a contract:

If the student expresses anger in a constructive way without using a swear word for three consecutive days; the teacher and student will meet with the PE teacher to recommend a probationary reinstatement in the regular education physical education class.

Coordinate a Cost-Response Program. Cost-response involves give and take. Appropriate behaviors earn "points." When the behaviors are inappropriate or out of control, there is a cost or loss of points. All behaviors are specifically identified and costs are clearly described in writing and orally.

Incorporate a Token Economy. Points are earned for good behavior. The points can be spent on items or activities identified as "valuable" to the student. The student is involved in setting the menu of reinforcements. The teacher generally determines the cost for each item.

Use Overcorrection. Overcorrection can be used effectively (but sparingly) in establishing behavior that is expected for such things as walking in the hallway, entering a classroom, or addressing a teacher politely. This type of repetition should be done cautiously and on a limited basis. Students who recognize inappropriate behavior respond more favorably to the repeat request.

No one behavior plan works for all students or all the time. It will be necessary to have a repertoire of options. Keep data on the effectiveness of the intervention. Data might include documenting the frequency (how often?), severity (how intense?), or the duration (how long?) of the behavior. The use of data supports changing a behavior plan if it is not working.

Document and Collect Data

Charting student behaviors will provide the teacher with the necessary data to make informed decisions. Not all behaviors can be changed at once. Select the behavior of real concern. Define the behavior clearly and in a way that can be measured. Table 3.2, Defining the Problem, identifies examples of specific language.

Table 3.2 Defining the Problem

Ambiguous Terms	Specific, Measurable Language
"Shena never has work done!"	"Shena's math homework has not been turned in for the past seven days. In science and social studies, 80 percent of the time, she turns in her papers one day after they are due."
"Jose is always late to class."	"During first hour, Jose has missed the first ten minutes of class for 14 of the last 20 days."
"Phyllis throws fits about everything."	"Phyllis starts to cry loudly and rocks back and forth when I ask her to put her materials away so we can transition from one subject to the next or when we move from our room to other locations."
"Tevon picks on everyone."	"Tevon stands in front of students who are smaller than he is and tells them 'Move! Or get beat up!'"

There are different types of data charts used for documenting student behaviors. The data recorded and type of chart depends on the behavior. It may be important to keep an interval or event count where you identify the percent of time the behavior occurs in a day, during one period, or during the morning or afternoon. Jose's tardy behavior above is best recorded on a *frequency chart* which provides a simple count. For Tevon, you might use a frequency chart and a *narrative record* of the antecedent—what happened before the behavior, during the behavior, and the consequence. *Duration recording* tracks how long a behavior lasts by noting start and end times, *and intensity charting* identifies the severity of the behavior when compared to normal behaviors. Phyllis's tantrums may require a duration chart or documentation of intensity. A variety of behaviors can be documented using Table 3.3 Frequency Count and Narrative Recording or Table 3.4 Ten Minute Observation—Interval Event Recording.

Table 3.3   Frequency Count and Narrative Recording

Student: _____ Date: _____

Time Observation Began: _____ Time Observation Ended: _____

Behavior of Concern: _____

Setting: _____ Activity: _____

Number of Times the Behavior Occurred (place a slash mark in the area)

Narrative Recording

What was the antecedent of the student's behavior? Describe what preceded or appeared to cause the behavior.

What was the consequence of the student's behavior? Describe what happened after or as a result of the behavior.

Table 3.4 Ten Minute Observation—Interval Event Recording

(What percentage of time does the behavior occur?)

Date: _____ Time: _____

Setting: _____

Student: _____

Task: _____

Intervals (one minute)	Compare the student with a peer	On Task Yes No	Off-task behavior: Circle Verbal Motor Passive	Comments: (e.g., What was the teacher doing?)
1	Student	Y N	V M P	
	Peer	Y N	V M P	
2	Student	Y N	V M P	
	Peer	Y N	V M P	
3	Student	Y N	V M P	
	Peer	Y N	V M P	
4	Student	Y N	V M P	
	Peer	Y N	V M P	
5	Student	Y N	V M P	
	Peer	Y N	V M P	
6	Student	Y N	V M P	
	Peer	Y N	V M P	
7	Student	Y N	V M P	
	Peer	Y N	V M P	
8	Student	Y N	V M P	
	Peer	Y N	V M P	
9	Student	Y N	V M P	
	Peer	Y N	V M P	
10	Student	Y N	V M P	
	Peer	Y N	V M P	

Percent of time on-task: ____/10 = ___%

Percent of off-task behavior in each area: ___%V   ___%M   ___%P

How does this compare with the peer? _____

Reinforce Positive Behavior

The goal of interventions is to increase positive behaviors. Reinforcing appropriate behaviors increases the chance that the behavior will be repeated. Recognize success and celebrate it immediately. Don't just say "Good job." Tell the student exactly what was done well. This is especially important when a student is first being taught a new skill. For example, if the goal is to increase the use of polite language, be specific: "Natalie, when you said 'PLEASE stop singing,' you were being polite because you said 'please.'" The statement reinforces the behavior to be repeated. It confirms the teacher's investment in the student's learning. Notice small efforts and resist comparing the student to others.

Some teachers mistakenly think reinforcing positive behaviors means offering a movie or popcorn every Friday. A better option is to have a student select a personally motivating activity when a goal has been achieved. Weekly classroom events that are not tied to academic or behavioral achievements may be reinforcing inappropriate behaviors of students who change "just enough" or "just in time" to participate.

Avoid Reinforcing Negative Behavior

If a student on an IEP exhibits extreme behavior, there may be a tendency to suggest the student be sent to the principal's office detention or suspended. This could be a temporary fix, but most often it does nothing to address the issues that caused the meltdown or standoff in the classroom. In many cases, removing the student from a classroom is positive reinforcement for negative behavior. In other words, the student may be getting exactly what he or she wants (Maag, 2001). The negative behavior has been reinforced, and chances are it will be repeated in the future with the same result.

Behaviors that worsen suggest a change and more intensive intervention may be needed. Some behaviors require a team meeting to determine different goals, a change in placement, or some other legal recourse.

Address Legal Requirements

Students who are on IEPs are entitled to legal rights and due process. They are not, however, given a free ride to do as they wish and get away with it. Determination of a disability and placement into special education means there has been agreement by a team on the identification of the behaviors that are associated with the disability. In addition, present levels of educational performance and issues attributed to a particular student's disability are documented, including the frequency, duration, or intensity of the student's behaviors. Over the years, clarification has been made regarding the behavior of students on IEPs and disciplinary procedures identified in school handbooks.

Keep in mind the following:

1. A Functional Behavioral Assessment (FBA) can and should be conducted any time a behavior is disruptive to the student or a class.

2. Students on an IEP can be suspended. However, by law, the number of days for suspensions during the year is limited to a total of ten. Behavior that warrants more than ten days must be addressed through an FBA.

3. The FBA is designed to review the specific behaviors associated with the infraction. The behavior is discussed to ensure a unified understanding. A team looks for an explanation, including underlying reasons the behavior occurred. More appropriate responses along with supports are determined, implemented, and evaluated. If there is not a Behavior Intervention Plan (BIP) in the IEP, one is written.

4. The BIP establishes student expectations, effective behavioral supports to be provided by the school, appropriate ways to de-escalate behaviors, and methods to evaluate the success of the plan.

5. Students on an IEP can be expelled. However, the expulsion would be considered a change in placement. It is not handled arbitrarily by a principal but must be considered through a Manifestation Determination meeting.

6. Manifestation Determination is a process initiated when a student on an IEP has broken a school rule. First, a team decision is made as to whether the IEP had been correctly implemented. Then the team determines if the behavior was caused by the disability. If it was, the team must then determine if the placement or IEP goals must be changed due to the severity of the infraction.

7. Mediation involves a third party who is appointed to listen to both sides in a dispute. The mediator moves between the parties, who are in separate locations. A compromise is generally reached based on the input.

8. Arbitration using a third party to make a decision may be necessary during a disagreement.

9. Conciliation provides an opportunity to bring two sides (parents and school districts) together to resolve issues amicably.

10. When a student becomes violent, physical restraint may be necessary. This involves a holding technique that requires specific training.

When situations require intensive interventions, secure the help of an administrator and implement the process with integrity to avoid legal ramifications.

Contingency Plans

Field trips or emergencies (including fire drills, evacuations caused by natural disasters or threats) may prompt a student's behavior to escalate. It is helpful to have a contingency plan to address student behaviors in unique situations. Depending on the student or the circumstance special educators may need to:

- Have people available for support,
- Carry a walkie-talkie, or
- Prepare the student for changes in a schedule.

The goal of any management plan is to teach the student acceptable behavior that can be maintained across settings.

Level Three: Maintaining Appropriate Behaviors

Students with disabilities can and should be taught self-management strategies. As students recognize and take control of their behaviors, they begin to make the transition from dependence to independence. Individuals with disabilities experience more success when taught to self-manage behaviors. For some students, the act of charting behavior provides a visual that reinforces positive growth. When students are involved in setting challenging but attainable goals, they more often value the outcome. There is a higher likelihood the behavior will be successfully maintained.

Self-Advocacy

Self-advocacy skills include age-appropriate strategies that are proactive. This is the opposite of "learned helplessness," or behavior that accompanies years of under-expectations or lack of training and accountability. Learned helplessness may appear as manipulation, "smooth talk," resistance, or denial.

Students who self-advocate are able to ask for assistance. Students with disabilities benefit from successful engagement in skills for the twenty-first century. Selecting and maintaining behaviors aligned with competencies, and including those personal and social skills that are necessary on a daily basis, is an effective professional practice. As a special education teacher, it is important to guide students in setting goals that are both specific to the student and universally applicable. This is also known as generalization.

Plan for Success

When working with students with disabilities, the overarching goal is to create opportunities for success and increase independence. All students benefit from quality instruction that prepares them for further academic work but also provides for the transition skills necessary to function well in society. The legislative mandate that students will achieve at high levels and be competitive in a world market is laudable and creates opportunities for all. Students with disabilities also need to be specifically taught skills that provide for success in future employment. If the discrepancy between academic and functional skills is too great, acting-out behaviors may occur.

Align IEP Goals with Twenty-First Century Skills

A helpful guide to use in planning for student success beyond the schoolhouse is a report published by the Secretary's Commission on Achieving Necessary Skills (SCANS). The US Departments of Labor and Education formed SCANS to study the kinds of competencies and skills workers must have to succeed in the workplace. The results of the study were published in a document titled *What Work Requires of Schools: A SCANS Report for America 2000* (US Department of Labor, 1991). Skills identified in the report can be used as IEP goals because they are relevant, identify positive behaviors, and support future success. The five SCANS competency areas are as follows:

1. *Resources.* Identify, organize, plan, and allocate resources, including
   - time,
   - money,
   - material and facilities,
   - human resources.

2. *Interpersonal.* Work with others in ways such as
   - participating as member of a team,
   - teaching others new skills,
   - serving clients or customers,
   - exercising leadership,
   - negotiating,
   - working with diversity.

3. *Information.* Be prepared to
   - acquire and evaluate information,
   - organize and maintain information,
   - interpret and communicate information,
   - use computers to process information.

4. *Systems.* Understand complex interrelationships including
   - monitoring and correcting performance.

5. *Technology.* Work with a variety of technology areas including
   - selecting technology,
   - applying technology to task,
   - maintaining and troubleshooting equipment.

The SCANS report also identifies basic skills, thinking skills, and personal qualities consistent with academic standards.

Basic Skills

- *Reading*—locates, understands, and interprets written information in prose and in documents such as manuals, graphs, and schedules

- *Writing*—communicates thoughts, ideas, information, and messages in writing; creates documents such as letters, directions, manuals, reports, graphs, and flow charts
- *Arithmetic/mathematics*—performs basic computations and approaches practical problems by choosing appropriately from a variety of mathematical techniques
- *Listening*—receives, attends to, interprets, and responds to verbal messages and other cues
- *Speaking*—organizes ideas and communicates orally

Thinking Skills

- *Creative thinking*—generates new ideas
- *Decision making*—specifies goals and constraints, generates alternatives, considers risks, and evaluates and chooses best alternatives
- *Problem solving*—recognizes problems and devises and implements plan of action
- *Visualizing*—organizes and processes symbols
- *Knowing how to learn*—uses efficient learning techniques to acquire and apply new knowledge and skills
- *Reasoning*—discovers a rule or principle underlying the relationship between two or more objects and applies it when solving a problem

Personal Qualities

- *Responsibility*—exerts a high level of effort and perseveres toward goal attainment
- *Self-esteem*—believes in own self-worth and maintains a positive view of self
- *Sociability*—demonstrates understanding, friendliness, adaptability, empathy, and politeness in group settings
- *Self-management*—assesses self accurately, sets personal goals, monitors progress, and exhibits self-control
- *Integrity/honesty*—chooses ethical courses of action

The professional responsibility of a special education teacher includes offering quality input in IEP discussions to ensure meaningful goals and relevant education for a student. Incorporating these twenty-first-century skills in IEPs can support and reinforce positive student behaviors for success now and in the future.

SUMMARY

Chapter 3 provides insight into three levels of managing student behavior. A teacher who practices prevention strategies can eliminate negative behaviors from occurring. Intervention with a student is designed to decrease specific behaviors that interfere with education. Maintaining appropriate behaviors requires involving the student in setting goals and designing instruction that has long-term benefits. In spite of sometimes difficult and complex situations, special educators are guided by legal requirements and professional ethics when managing student behaviors.

SELF-ASSESSMENT AND REFLECTION

After reading Chapter 3, please reflect on your knowledge and skill.

Self-Assessment Items

Respond to the following by answering Yes, Somewhat, or No.

I am able to

_____ 1. Analyze classroom management needs,

_____ 2. Discuss the three levels used to manage student behaviors,

_____ 3. Identify effective practices for preventing inappropriate student behaviors,

_____ 4. Identify practices that increase positive student behaviors,

_____ 5. Determine effective interventions when inappropriate student behavior occurs,

_____ 6. Identify skills and behaviors students need to successfully prepare for the future,

_____ 7. Discuss legal rights and professional ethics that guide work with students.

Reflection

1. Which of the self-assessment items do you feel fully competent in?

2. Which of the self-assessment items do you feel needs some more work, emphasis, or study time?

3. Identify two specific actions you can take to enrich and strengthen your instructional effectiveness.

4

four—cuatro—plaub

Designing Effective Instruction

OBJECTIVES

1. Describe the six parts of a comprehensive lesson plan.

2. Define and write content objectives and language objectives.

3. Explain the difference between a teaching strategy and a learning activity.

4. Describe the lesson's instructional sequence.

5. Describe the nine components of the ABC Assessment Tool.

Effective instruction leads to increased student learning, achievement, and success. Effective instruction involves a multitude of teacher decisions that are based on professional standards and the teacher's interwoven attributes of knowledge, attitude, teaching and learning preference, behavior, and skill.

There are several elements leading to effective instruction but two of the most important factors are substantial planning and detailed reflection. Substantial planning is necessary to determine many items, such as the lesson's targeted standards and objectives, the delivery method(s), and the necessary instructional materials and resources. Detailed reflection provides the opportunity for the teacher to determine the strengths and limitations of the lesson and, most importantly, make future lesson decisions that promote highly effective lessons.

This chapter is designed to provide the reader with information, strategies, and skills leading to effective instruction.

WISDOM OF PRACTICE: MR. RODRIQUEZ MAKES A PLAN

Mr. Rodriquez, the middle school special education teacher, decided to take a vacation during his school's spring-break time. He pondered for a while, did his research, and decided on a wonderful destination. He then had to determine the best method of travel—car, train, or air. Regarding his travel, Mr. Rodriquez had another difficult decision. Should he spend his time traveling slower (by train or car) and enjoying the travel sights along the way, or should he travel faster (air) and enjoy the final destination longer?

Likewise, Mr. Rodriquez has similar decisions to make in his special education classroom on a daily basis. With his instruction, he must first decide on the students' learning destination—we'll call those learner objectives. Next, instead of his travel method, Mr. Rodriquez must decide on the most effective instructional method to efficiently and effectively get his students to their learning destination. In some cases, the travel time (process) is the most important element of the instruction. In other cases it may be less important, and the academic product becomes the key element. The decision is based on how Mr. Rodriquez sees the balance for his students between process and product.

IN BRIEF: WHAT DOES THE RESEARCH SAY?

In terms of effective instructional strategies, the Mid-continent Research for Education and Learning (McREL) has stated, "Research tells us that one key trait of effective teachers is their use of instructional strategies that work" (2000). As a result of more than 30 years of research McREL has identified nine strategies (Table 4.1) that "have the greatest likelihood of positively affecting student achievement" (McREL, 2000).

In addition, the knowledge and skills needed to design effective instruction correlate well with the work of the Interstate New Teacher Assessment and Support Consortium and the Council for Exceptional Children (CEC).

Table 4.1	Categories of Instructional Strategies that Strongly Affect Student Achievement
Category	**Definition**
Identifying similarities and differences	Helping students compare, classify, and create metaphors and analogies
Summarizing and note taking	Helping students analyze, sift through, and synthesize information in order to decide which new information is most important to record and remember
Reinforcing effort and providing recognition	Teaching students about the role that effort can play in enhancing achievement, and recognizing students for working toward an identified level of performance

Category	Definition
Homework and practice	Providing students with opportunities to learn new information and skills and to practice skills they have recently learned
Nonlinguistic representations	Helping students generate nonlinguistic representations of information, including graphic organizers, pictures and pictographs, mental pictures, concrete representations, and kinesthetic activity
Cooperative learning	Creating opportunities for students to develop positive interdependence, face-to-face interaction, individual and group accountability, interpersonal and small-group skills, and group processing
Setting goals and providing feedback	Helping students set their own learning goals in order to establish direction and providing students with timely feedback about their progress
Generating and testing hypotheses	Helping students generate and test hypotheses through a variety of tasks, through systems-analysis, problem-solving, historical investigation, invention, experimental inquiry, and decision-making
Activating prior knowledge	Helping students retrieve what they already know about a topic

www.mcrel.org/PDF/Instruction/5992TG_What_Works.pdf

The Interstate New Teacher Assessment and Support Consortium (INTASC), a consortium of state education agencies and national educational organizations, have developed ten *model "core" standards* for what all beginning teachers should know, be like, and be able to do in order to practice responsibly, regardless of the subject matter or grade level being taught. Specific INTASC information can be found at the Council of Chief State School Officers Web page at www.ccsso.org/projects/Interstate_New_ Teacher_Assessment_and_ Support_Consortium.

The work of INTASC is guided by one basic premise: An effective teacher (general education, special education, or other area) must be able to integrate content knowledge with the specific strengths and needs of students to assure that *all* students learn and perform at high levels.

Special educators are aware of the alignment of the CEC Standard Domain Areas to the INTASC standards. The CEC Professional Standards for Preparation and Licensure address knowledge and skills required of highly qualified special education teachers. *What Every Special Educator Must Know: Ethics, Standards, and Guidelines for Special Educators* (2008) can be downloaded at http://www.cec.sped.org/Content/ NavigationMenu/ProfessionalDevelopment/ProfessionalStandards/?from=tlcHome.

A brief analysis of CEC standards that identify the special education teacher's responsibilities in lesson design compared with INTASC standards is found in Table 4.2.

Each one of the ten INTASC standards is a vitally important component of effective instruction. However, this chapter will focus primarily on INTASC Standard 3: *The*

Table 4.2 INTASC Standards and CEC Standards

INTASC Core Principles	CEC Standard Domain Areas
Standard 2: Student Learning: The teacher understands how children learn and develop, and can provide learning opportunities that support their intellectual, social, and personal development.	*Development and Characteristics of Learners:* The nature of a student's disability requires special educators to: Use their knowledge of exceptionalities to develop opportunities to learn, interact socially, and participate in the community.
Standard 3: Diverse Learners: The teacher understands how students differ in their approaches to learning and creates instructional opportunities that are adapted to diverse learners.	*Individual Learning Differences:* The nature of a student's disability requires special educators to: Provide meaningful and challenging learning opportunities based on the unique needs. Actively seek ways to connect primary language, culture, and family background to individualize instruction.
Standard 4: Instructional Strategies: The teacher understands and uses a variety of instructional strategies to encourage students' development of critical thinking, problem solving and performance skills.	*Instructional Strategies:* The nature of a student's disability requires special educators to: Consider special and general education curriculum, adapting and modifying when needed. Promote and document critical thinking, problem solving, and performance skills in a variety of settings.
Standard 5: Learning Environment: The teacher uses an understanding of individual and group motivation and behavior to create a learning environment that encourages positive social interaction, active engagement in learning, and self-motivation.	*Learning Environments and Social Interaction:* The nature of a student's disability requires special educators to: Help general education teachers include students with disabilities in the classroom, and involve the student in meaningful learning activities and positive social interactions with peers. Create learning environments that promote cultural understanding, safety, and emotional well being, and active engagement.

Standard 6: Communication: The teacher uses knowledge of effective verbal, nonverbal, and media communication techniques to foster active inquiry, collaboration, and supportive interaction in the classroom.	*Language:* The nature of a student's disability requires special educators to: Use individualized strategies and technologies to enhance language development and communication skills. Provide language models and use communication strategies and resources to effectively teach content and skills to students with disabilities whose primary language is not English.
Standard 7: Planning Instruction: The teacher plans instruction based on knowledge of subject matter, students, the community, and curriculum goals.	*Instructional Planning:* The nature of a student's disability requires special educators to: Systematically identify goals and objectives based on the needs and abilities. Design and model explicit instruction to ensure acquisition and generalization.
Standard 8: Assessment and Evaluation: The teacher understands and uses formal and informal assessment strategies to evaluate and ensure the continuous intellectual, social, and physical development of the learner.	*Assessment:* The nature of a student's disability requires special educators to: Implement and adjust instruction in response to ongoing learning progress. Conduct formal and informal assessments of behavior, academic achievement, and the learning environment and experiences in order to support the achievement of students with disabilities.

teacher understands how students differ in their approaches to learning and creates instructional opportunities that are adapted to diverse learners

Effective instruction starts with effective planning. One of the most important steps in planning an effective lesson is knowing and understanding the critical instructional planning elements and questions. This chapter will identify the components of a comprehensive lesson plan.

Prior to completing a comprehensive lesson plan, it is imperative that classroom teachers have an accurate knowledge of their students' academic, social/emotional, and language abilities.

Teachers should check with the school's resources for assistance in gaining more in-depth knowledge concerning their students' learning needs and abilities. Many schools now employ English language learner (ELL) specialists, special education and related service specialists, and gifted and talented specialists to assist classroom teachers in better understanding the proficiencies and needs of the students for which they are advocates. Often, these specialists have previously conducted various assessments with the students and are therefore able to offer high-quality instructional advice.

PROFESSIONAL PRACTICE

Effective planning is an essential component of successful teaching at every academic level and will increase both the competence and confidence of the teacher. This will lead to more successful student learning. Effective planning implies that all students will be targeted for the instruction, meaning that some students may receive a different educational experience than other students in the class. Some students might move through the instruction at a pace different from other students. This type of lesson planning is often referred to as differentiated instruction. Some lessons may require significant differentiation, others little or no differentiation.

The Lesson Plan—An Overview

While there are many different recognized lesson plan formats, the following lesson plan pays special attention to planning for individual learning differences. This comprehensive lesson plan has six distinct parts. Each part provides significant information considered necessary for effective classroom instruction.

Part 1: Basic Information

1. Day and Date
2. Class Name and Grade
3. Lesson Name

Part 2: Student Learning

1. Content Standard
2. Content Objective
3. Language Objective
4. Key Vocabulary

Part 3: Student Diversity

1. Learning Styles (Preferences)
2. Cognitive Progression
3. Language Domain

Part 4: Instructional Sequence

1. Lesson Starting
2. Direct Teaching
3. Student Activity
4. Lesson Ending

Part 5: Instructional Materials

1. Print
2. Nonprint
3. Technology

Part 6: Lesson Assessment and Evaluation

1. Authentic, Bias Free, Constructivist
2. Developmental, Embedded, Focused
3. Generalizable, High in Rigor, Interesting

The Lesson Plan—Part 1: Basic Information

Every lesson plan should contain three basic lesson items.

1. Day and Date: Experienced teachers report that many of their lessons are more effective on some days of the week and less effective on other days. By knowing and tracking the lesson's day and date, a teacher can use this information when the specific lesson may be repeated in subsequent school terms or years. It's possible the teacher can make this lesson more effective by conducting the lesson on a different day and/or date.

2. Class Name and Grade: Identifying the lesson by class name (Algebra 1, Geography, Anatomy, Poetry) and grade (5, 8, 10) will enable the teacher to arrange and categorize his/her lessons in an orderly fashion.

3. Lesson Name: Every lesson should have a unique name. The name should specifically identify that lesson. Do not use names that are typically "unit" or "generic" names such as fractions, respiration, oceans, or punctuation. Instead, the lessons might be named "Adding Fractions With Like Denominators," "Respiratory Anatomy," "Oceans Introduction," or "Punctuation: The Comma."

The Lesson Plan—Part 2: Student Learning

Content Standard

First and foremost, as stated in INTASC Standard #1, "Teachers must have a thorough understanding of the central concepts, tools of inquiry, and structures of the discipline he or she teaches." This means, among other things, that the teacher has a clear understanding of the content standards of the course so that individual lessons leading to the students' achievement of the content standard can be developed.

In many instances, content standards can be found in the corresponding national education standards. National content standards are typically developed and identified for most K–12 disciplines by the national organizations, associations, or councils representing the specific discipline.

Examples:

National Council for the Social Studies (www.ncss.org)

National Council of Teachers of English (www.ncte.org)

National Council of Teachers of Mathematics (www.nctm.org)

National Science Teachers Association (www.nsta.org)

Other national education groups also offer important standards connected to student learning.

Examples:

Council for Exceptional Children (www.cec.sped.org)

Teachers of English to Speakers of Other Languages, Inc. (www.tesol.org)

In addition to the national content standards, individual states often require or recommend additional learning standards. Going one step further, some local school districts may also require additional learning standards.

Many national and state standards are written in a global sense.

Example 1:

Social Studies: "Learners [will] understand the world in spatial terms and possess knowledge of places and regions, physical systems, and the interactions of environment and society. In addition, learners need the ability to map information in a spatial context and to interpret such maps." (www.socialstudies.org/standards/strands)

Example 2

Health Education: "Students will demonstrate the ability to access valid information and products and services to enhance health." (www.cdc.gov/healthyyouth/sher/standards/)

Each of these two examples will probably require a significant amount of instructional time to assure student achievement of the standard. Each standard would require the teacher to develop several smaller learning segments leading to the full completion, and achievement, of the standard.

Therefore, due to the comprehensiveness of the standards, teachers must break down the standard into smaller learning segments, each segment leading to the full completion (and achievement) of the content standard. Sometimes these smaller learning segments are called substandards, benchmarks, or performance indicators. It is these smaller learning segments that form the basis and foundation of the lesson plan.

Learner objectives at the lesson plan level are critical. Learner objectives provide and direct both the process and product of learning for both the teacher and his or her students. However, some teachers make the common mistake of preparing instructional objectives thinking they are learner objectives. Instructional objectives are intrinsically different from learner objectives.

Learner objectives clearly define what the student is expected to know and/or be able to do as a result of his or her participation in the lesson.

Instructional objectives, often called teacher objectives, customarily define what the teacher will do in the class, such as take attendance, hand out assignment sheets, give a lecture/demonstration, assign student small groups, and collect materials.

This lesson plan section will focus on two types of learner objectives—content objectives and language objectives. Both content and language objectives are essential components of the lesson plan and effective instruction. Learner objectives directly guide the teacher's instructional strategies and the students' learning activities.

Teaching strategies refer to the structure, system, methods, techniques, procedures, and processes that a teacher uses during instruction. These are strategies the *teacher* employs to assist student learning.

Learning activities refer to the teacher-guided instructional tasks or assignments for students. These are the academic learning activities that the *student* works on in and out of class.

Content and Language Objectives

Content and language objectives define and describe the very specific learning that is expected at the end of the daily lesson. The important element here is at the end of the *daily* lesson. Content and language objectives, from a lesson perspective, should reflect a relatively short learning time span. At the lesson level, content and language objectives will probably be much more detailed than a longer learning time span such as in chapter, unit, section, or course objectives.

At the lesson level both content objectives and language objectives generally have five distinct characteristics. Objectives should always be:

1. clear (obvious and understandable),

2. concise (brief, to the point),

3. attainable (reasonable, achievable),

4. relevant (useful, pertinent, interesting), and

5. measurable (assessable, quantifiable).

All students in the classroom should have the opportunity to *see* and *hear* their content and language objectives *prior* to instruction, and they should also have an opportunity to *ask* any clarifying questions they may have about their learning objectives. Teachers consistently report that students who have these opportunities are more apt to achieve the objectives than students who do not have the opportunity to see, hear, and ask questions about their learning expectations.

Content Objectives

Content objectives define the essential targeted knowledge and/or skill of the discipline (Rohwer & Wandberg, 2005). Content objectives, as mentioned previously, are commonly derived from national and/or state standards. Basically, they define the important facts, concepts, and/or skills of the discipline (such as math, science, social studies, health). Content objectives should be written at the lesson-plan level and written in student language.

Example 1

After listening to the first chapter of *The Red Badge of Courage,* the student will accurately recall three important details about the main character.

Example 2

The student will correctly identify four road hazard signs on a practice test in preparation for the driver's license exam.

Language Objectives

Language objectives define the language skills needed to make the content objectives understandable to the learners. Language objectives are critical for English Language Learners (ELL) and many special education students. Language objectives clearly describe what the students will be able to do (relative to the content) while using English. Language objectives focus on one or more of four language domains:

1. Reading

2. Writing

3. Listening

4. Speaking

Example 1

Accurately label and orally describe four concepts of the rain cycle using the voice-activated computer animation software.

Example 2

Write five safety rules that must be followed in the science classroom.

Key Vocabulary

Many lessons consist of key vocabulary necessary for full student comprehension of the content objectives and/or the language objectives. Most academic content areas have a unique associated vocabulary. The important terms and expressions used in one content area are often significantly different from those in another content area. For example, consider the important terms and expressions commonly used in math, social studies, science, language arts, health, and music. All of these terms are either unique or multiple-meaning terms.

A term such as "numerator" is considered content specific. On the other hand, a term such as "scale" is considered a multiple-meaning term. Can you give an example of how the following content areas might define "scale"?

- Music
- Art
- Geography
- Biology
- Health

This example of the term "scale" is precisely why *language objectives* are critical in today's classrooms.

For a student with limited or low English language proficiency, multiple meaning terms can be highly confusing. This is especially true, for example, when the student hears, correctly, the term used in the context of science in a course at the beginning of the day. Then, later that same day, the identical term is used, also correctly, in the context of geography. Multiple-meaning terms should be acknowledged as having multiple meanings. When listing the lesson's key vocabulary, as a reminder, it is often a good idea to circle the multiple-meaning terms.

The Lesson Plan—Part 3: Student Diversity

From multiple dimensions (such as cultural, language, cognitive ability), classrooms across the United States are becoming more diverse. This diversity creates an enormous challenge for most classroom teachers—to find an effective and successful approach to teaching that takes into account the student diversity in their classrooms. Consider for a moment the multiple student disabilities that are eligible to receive special education services. Add to that the growing number of English language learners, some of which may also qualify for special education services. Then add the number of students who are identified as "on-level," and, finally, add the approximately six percent of students who are identified as gifted and/or talented. All of these students may be in one classroom!

Three items should be recorded and tracked in an effective lesson plan:

1. Learning Styles

2. Cognitive Progression

3. Language Domain

Learning Styles

Student learning styles, sometimes referred to as learning preferences, vary greatly. Rarely can a single lesson plan address the learning styles of all students in the class. However, over the course of a few days, many learning styles could, and should, be emphasized and supported.

Dr. Howard Gardner developed a model of multiple learning styles in 1983. Dr. Gardner, a professor of education at Harvard University, suggests eight different learning preferences (Gardner, 1983).

1. *Verbal-Linguistic*—prefers attention to words, language, and syntax in most any form such as reading, hearing, seeing words, speaking, writing, discussion, and debating.

2. *Math-Logic*—prefers working with patterns and relationships, classifying, problem-solving, and reasoning.

3. *Spatial*—prefers working with pictures, colors, maps, puzzles, drawing, charts, and visualization.

4. *Bodily-Kinesthetic*—prefers athletics, dancing, using tools, moving, touching, acting, and crafts.

5. *Musical*—prefers singing, rhythm, listening to music, and melodies.

6. *Interpersonal*—prefers sharing, cooperating, communicating, and interviewing.

7. *Intrapersonal*—prefers working alone, understanding self, reflecting, and doing self-paced projects and activities.

8. *Naturalist*—prefers working in nature, exploring, and learning about the natural plant and animal environment.

By documenting the lesson plan's primary learning style, the teacher will be able to keep an accurate record of the various learning styles covered over time. Teachers are encouraged to provide a variety of learning preference activities.

Cognitive Progression

Cognitive progression refers to the level of thinking, or the level of rigor, the teacher is asking of his or her students. The cognitive domain involves the development of intellectual skills.

This part of the lesson plan clearly identifies the students' target cognitive level(s). Lessons, over time, should challenge each student's cognitive level of thinking. Students progress at varying rates as they strive to achieve higher-order thinking skills.

Still being used today is the information of cognitive progression developed by Benjamin Bloom. Over 50 years ago, Dr. Bloom headed a group of educational psychologists who developed a classification of levels of intellectual behavior important in learning (Bloom, Engelhart, Furst, Hill, & Krathwohl, 1956). The six levels of intellectual behavior listed from low level to high level are: Knowledge, Comprehension, Application, Analysis, Synthesis, and Evaluation. Over the years, many models representing Dr. Bloom's taxonomy of cognitive progression have been developed. Figure 4.1 represents a simple illustration of the cognitive progression.

Figure 4.1	Cognitive Progression

Low   >>>>>>   Intellectual Behavior   >>>>>>   High

Knowledge > Comprehension > Application > Analysis > Synthesis > Evaluation

Teachers who learn and appropriately use the common verbs associated with each level of student learning objectives will be able to more accurately target students' specific levels of cognitive thinking.

Sample learning verbs associated with each cognitive level include the following:

Knowledge: being able to remember an idea or fact in a form very close to the way it was first encountered.

    a. To name: to use the name or title by which an object, person, or idea is usually designated.

    b. To define: to give the precise meaning of a word or term

    c. To list: to itemize, to record a number of things or persons of a like nature

Comprehension: being able to represent an understanding of the literal message contained in a communication.

    a. *To identify:* to discover the nature or special characteristics of something

    b. *To explain:* to clarify the meaning or to offer reasons for or a cause of something

    c. *To describe:* to give a detailed account of something

    d. *To distinguish:* to recognize as being different or distinctive from otherwise similar things.

Application: being able to demonstrate abstractions such as theories, principles, ideas, rules, and methods for the solution of a problem.

    a. *To interpret:* to classify a meaning by restating an idea or theory in another way.

    b. *To illustrate:* to clarify an idea or theory by using examples or comparisons.

    c. *To predict:* to declare what will happen at a later time.

    d. *To translate:* to put in simpler terms or to convey from one form to another.

Analysis: being able to break down a theory or plan into its separate parts and determining the relationship of those parts and how they are organized; also the techniques used to convey the meaning or establish the conclusions of a communication.

    a. *To analyze:* to separate into parts so as to determine the nature of the whole.

    b. *To classify:* to sort things or ideas according to a set of shared characteristics.

    c. *To categorize:* to determine the placement of an idea or object in a specified division of a classification system.

    d. *To differentiate:* to note or demonstrate characteristics establishing the uniqueness of a thing or idea.

Synthesis: being able to put new elements and parts together so as to form a new pattern or structure not clearly there before.

    a. *To synthesize:* to combine data or information so as to form a new or more complex product.

    b. *To conclude:* to reach a decision or form an opinion about something following careful study of a problem or issue.

    c. *To propose:* to put forward a plan or an idea for consideration, discussion, or acceptance.

Evaluation: being able to make judgments about the worth of ideas, works, and solutions. (The criteria may be quantitative, qualitative, or both.)

    a. *To evaluate:* to examine and judge the worth or value of something.

    b. *To compare:* to examine in order to note similarities among or between things.

    c. *To contrast:* to show how one thing is strikingly different from another or others.

    d. *To appraise:* to estimate the quality, amount, size, or other features of an object or product.

The important idea to remember when developing the lesson plan is to vary the cognitive rigor. Often the teacher may have to, or should, differentiate and target varying cognitive levels among his or her students in a single lesson.

Language Domains

Reading, writing, listening, and speaking are four primary language domains. As teachers develop lesson plans it is important that they identify the lesson's targeted language domain(s). As with the learning styles and cognitive progression, the lesson's language domain should be tracked over time to assure that all four language domains are being adequately addressed. The lesson's language objective(s) provide the specifics of the lesson's language domain.

The Lesson Plan—Part 4: Instructional Sequence

How a lesson starts, progresses, and concludes has an effect on the degree of student learning. Lessons that are delivered without sufficient planning can lead to student confusion, negative classroom behavior, and decreased learning. As you read in Chapter Three, there are many factors in managing a classroom. One of the primary factors supporting effective classroom management is a well-planned lesson.

Student discipline is one of several primary reasons reported by teachers who choose to leave the teaching profession early in their career. The National Education Association statistics indicate about 20 percent of all new teachers leave the classroom within three years. In urban districts, close to 50 percent of new teachers leave the classroom during their first five years (NEA, 2006).

Thoroughly prepared lesson plans can create a positive learning environment leading to improved student achievement. Four components should be considered in every lesson plan:

1. Starting the Lesson

2. Direct Teaching

3. Student Activity

4. Ending the Lesson

Starting the Lesson

The first few minutes of the lesson set the stage for the entire lesson. Teachers who are able to create content relevance and student excitement find that students are more motivated to become engaged in the lesson and in the learning process. Getting the students focused on the lesson's content and language objectives is critical. How do successful teachers get their students focused? Some use stories, anecdotes, local statistics, props, artifacts, videos, short games, self-assessments, or informational quizzes.

During this phase of instruction, the teacher's role is primarily that of a leader. The students' role is primarily active listening, observing, and participating. As you continue to read about the subsequent lesson plan components, you will notice that the suggested teacher and student roles change.

Direct Teaching

During the direct teaching lesson phase, the teacher, coteacher, or guest speaker is providing important content or process information. Teachers use direct teaching time to lecture, demonstrate, model, connect students to past learning or experiences, emphasize key vocabulary, and to question students.

Student Activity

Student activity time is often the time when students learn to become more independent learners. This is the time when students work to complete tasks. It is a time when students are able to make some learning and process decisions.

During this time, students may be working independently, with partners, and/or in small groups. Students are reading, writing, listening, and speaking. They are solving problems and making decisions. They are creating final products and performances. These final products and performances may take a variety of forms such as slide shows, surveys, written and oral reports, videos, debates, public service announcements (PSAs), displays, or skits.

The teacher's role during the student activity time now transitions from leader to more coaching and facilitating. The teacher is now asking questions, encouraging students, keeping students focused, and informally assessing student progress.

Ending the Lesson

As the name implies, this phase of the lesson summarizes, reviews, and puts closure to the lesson. Students are assessing the progress in both oral and written form. They are setting goals for future lessons. They are turning in assignments and returning all the materials used during the class. The teacher guides the lesson review, collects assignments, and provides other important announcements.

Next comes one of the more critical questions. How much class time should a teacher spend in each portion of the lesson plan? Although there may be several exceptions, many teachers find the following general guidelines helpful. However, when timing adjustments are necessary, it is recommended to keep the student activity phase at least 50 percent of the class time.

Example:

Lesson Phase	Total Class Time	50-Minute Class
Starting the Lesson	10%	5 minutes
Direct Teaching	20%	10 minutes
Student Activity	50%	25 minutes
Ending the Lesson	20%	10 minutes

The Lesson Plan—Part 5: Instructional Materials

Successful lessons often require an array of instructional materials. Instructional materials can be separated into three categories—print, nonprint, and technology.

1. Print materials commonly include items such as worksheets, quizzes/tests, self-assessments, pamphlets, and news articles.

2. Nonprint materials include items such as colored markers, scissors, tape, and glue. Also included in this category are items such as manipulatives, artifacts, models, manikins, and other hands-on types of materials.

3. Technology materials include items such as DVDs, CDs, camera, projectors, software, batteries, extra projection bulbs, and extension cords.

Many teachers find it helpful to make and use a prototype checklist for instructional materials needed for each lesson. See Table 4.3.

Table 4.3 Sample Instructional Materials Checklist

Lesson Title: _____

Date: _____

Instructional Materials	
Print	**Needed (√)**
Worksheets	
Quizzes/Tests	
Self-Assessments	
Pamphlets	
Books	
Newspapers/Magazines	
Transparencies	
Large Print or Adapted Texts	
Progress Monitoring Charts	
Posters With Standards/Expectations	
Other	
Nonprint	**Needed (√)**
Maps	
Globes	
Manipulatives	
Artifacts	

(Continued)

Table 4.3 (Continued)

Nonprint	Needed (√)
Models	
Manikins	
Props	
Experiment Equipment	
Clipboards	
Masking Tape	
Sticky Pads/Index Cards	
Pencils/Erasers/Staples/Rulers	
Pencil Grips	
Markers	
Other	
Technology	**Needed (√)**
Assistive Technology	
DVDs/CDs	
Camera/Video Camera	
Projectors/Extra Bulbs	
Calculators	
Spell Checkers	
Software	
Batteries	
Extension Cords	
TV/Monitor	
Computer/Computer Projection	
Overhead Projector	
Other	

The Lesson Plan—Part 6: Lesson Assessment and Evaluation

Lesson plans need to be assessed and evaluated. Suppose a middle school science teacher teaches three consecutive physical science classes the first three class periods of the day to similar groups of students. Many times the teacher will make a quick change to the lesson plan between the first and second period because he or she notices a necessary adjustment that will improve the lesson's effectiveness.

ABC TOOL

A consistent tool to assess and evaluate a lesson is helpful. The ABC Tool (Rohwer & Wandberg, 2001) is one method used to assess and evaluate a lesson. The ABC Tool consists of nine assessment elements starting with the first nine letters of the alphabet. Each item can be scored on a scale of low (1), medium (2), or high (3), indicating the degree each is present in the lesson.

A = Authentic

_____ The lesson represents how real people in the real world need or use this knowledge and/or skill.

B = Bias Free

_____ The lesson provides all students with an opportunity to learn and be successful.

C = Constructivist

_____ The lesson provides students with the opportunity to make decisions about how to demonstrate their learning and achievement.

_____ The lesson requires several teacher and/or student interactions.

D = Developmental

_____ The students in every class have the opportunity to hear and see (read) their content and language learning objectives prior to instruction.

_____ The students have an opportunity to ask clarifying questions about their learning objectives.

_____ The lesson's objectives are appropriate to the intellectual, physical, language development, and psychological maturity of the students.

_____ The lesson is part of a planned, scaffolded teaching strategy.

(Continued)

(Continued)

_____ The teacher's instructions are clear, concise, and appropriate for the students' proficiency.

_____ The lesson is linked to students' background and prior learning.

E = Embedded

_____ The lesson is an integral part of the school's content curriculum.

F = Focused

_____ The lesson stays on target to address and assess key content understandings and skills

_____ The lesson requires activities that integrate multiple language modalities such as reading, writing, listening, and speaking.

G = Generalizable

_____ The lesson's specific skills and knowledge represent the larger learning required for personal, family, and community.

H = High in Rigor

_____ The lesson represents high expectations for student learning.

I = Interesting

_____ The students enjoy and are interested in this lesson.

_____ The students are actively engaged in the lesson.

The maximum total score is 51. The items with the lowest scores should be targeted for improvement.

And, finally, no lesson assessment should be considered complete until the degree of student learning, achievement, and success has been accurately determined. See Chapter 8 for detailed information on student assessment and evaluation.

SUMMARY

An academically sound lesson design also has a significant influence on class management issues. Teachers should continuously monitor their lesson designs as they progress through the school year. They should frequently reflect and make notes on the effectiveness of their lessons. By doing this, the teacher will have valuable information on any adjustments that may be necessary to make the lesson more effective if and when the lesson would be used, modified, or adapted for another student or group of students.

SELF-ASSESSMENT AND REFLECTION

After reading Chapter 4, please reflect on your knowledge and skill.

Self-Assessment Items

Respond to the following by answering Yes, Somewhat, or No.

I am able to

_____ 1. Describe the six parts of a comprehensive lesson plan,

_____ 2. Define and write content objectives and language objectives,

_____ 3. Explain the difference between a teaching strategy and a learning activity,

_____ 4. Describe the lesson's instructional sequence,

_____ 5. Describe the nine components of the ABC Assessment Tool.

Reflection

1. Which of the self-assessment items do you feel fully competent in?

2. Which of the self-assessment items do you believe need some more work, emphasis, or study time?

3. Identify two specific actions you can take to enrich and strengthen your instructional effectiveness.

5

five—cinco—tsib

Teaching Strategies and Learning Activities

OBJECTIVES

1. Define and describe active student learning.

2. Describe various strategies to implement active student learning.

3. Describe potential strengths and limitations of selected student learning activities.

4. Identify several ways to overcome common obstacles related to the implementation of active student learning.

Many special education teachers and general education classroom teachers continue to organize their instruction around traditional methods. These traditional methods frequently involve students passively reading, independently completing worksheets, watching a video, asking questions, or listening and taking notes from a teacher's lecture.

Why do teachers continually use these traditional methods when there is strong evidence that student learning can be enhanced even more by using more engaging lessons and activities?

The purpose of this chapter will be to describe how teachers can develop and implement teaching strategies and learning activities that help students with a wide range of abilities be active and productive learners in the classroom. However, teachers should note that there are some specific obstacles associated with the use of active student learning activities.

WISDOM OF PRACTICE:
MS. WEBSTER GETS ACTIVE!

Ms. Webster is completing her second year as a middle school special education teacher. She is noticing an increase in her class management issues such as students talking during her lectures, more students asking to go to the bathroom or sharpen their pencils. Students were not completing assigned readings and worksheets. A couple of students recently told Ms. Webster that they were bored.

Ms. Webster, for the most part, was teaching in a very traditional manner. Her teaching consisted of her students listening to her lecture, reading the textbook, and completing the summary worksheets at the end of chapters. Her students had little or no opportunity for student-to-student or student-to-teacher interaction. Rarely did her students experience any instructional format other than whole-class instruction. They did not have opportunities to interact in small groups or with partners. They rarely had opportunities to solve problems, make decisions, or share any personal background information or experiences.

Feeling a soaring level of frustration, Ms. Webster asked a colleague to observe her class. Within a few days, following the observation and receiving recommendations from her colleague, Ms. Webster began to incorporate more active student learning in her classroom such as discovering, processing, applying, and evaluating content information. Ms. Webster's students were more academically attentive and actively involved in reading, writing, listening, and speaking activities.

Within a short period of time Ms. Webster was becoming quite competent in selecting and using active learning strategies that aligned with her lessons' content and language objectives.

IN BRIEF: WHAT DOES THE RESEARCH SAY?

Engaging students with disabilities in active learning creates both motivation and opportunity to learn. Researchers provide evidence that collaborative and interactive student participation, coupled with formative assessment, leads to student achievement (Bransford, Brown, & Cocking, 2000; Stiggins, 2001). Practices that elicit all students' active participation as well as their ability to think critically and creatively in order to communicate their learning provide snapshots to guide teacher instruction. Teachers are responsible for assuring that all students are productively engaged (Crawford, Schlager, Penuel, & Toyama, 2009) and making progress. Individual Education Programs (IEPs) provide the outline of what must be accomplished, but the teacher is the architect of meaningful learning opportunities connected to standards, goals, and objectives. Cognitive strategy instruction has been used effectively for students with learning disabilities to scaffold and improve writing (Hallenbeck, 2002). Research on active responding supports student achievement across content domains such as science and disability areas including autism (Carnahan, Musti-Rao, & Bailey, 2009; Maheady, Michielli-Pendl, Mallette, & Harper, 2002). Tasks designed to activate students connect them with content, peers, and tools of learning. Active learning can be used to maximize cognitive skills, incorporate social networks, enhance time on task, provide immediate and responsive feedback, and increase student accountability (Crawford, et al., 2009; Hinds, 2002).

PROFESSIONAL PRACTICE

Many teachers want to move beyond traditional methods of teaching. They want to find better instructional ways to engage students in learning. They want to find better instructional ways to involve their students in higher-order thinking and reasoning skills. They want to find better ways to create lessons that involve multiple, yet integrated, skills such as communication, problem solving, decision making, inquiry, and summarizing.

Active Student Learning Activities

Active student learning activities are hands-on tasks that take students out of their books, sometimes out of their seats, sometimes out of their classroom, sometimes out of their school, and out of their familiar ways of thinking and learning. Active student learning activities are intended to make students actively engaged through reading, writing, listening, and speaking. Active learning assists students in becoming responsible participants in their own learning and achievement.

Active student learning implies that students are doing more than simply listening or watching. It involves the instructional elements of reading, writing, listening, and speaking, and typically provides opportunities for students to use several of these four language domains.

Active Student Learning Obstacles

Incorporating active teaching strategies and learning activities into a classroom setting does not come easy for all teachers. Some teachers find implementing active student learning activities into their instruction a pleasant and exciting strategy, whereas other teachers are fearful, apprehensive, and even terrified when faced with the challenge of making active student learning a significant part of their instruction. There are several reasons why some teachers refuse to use, or even attempt, active student learning activities. Some common reasons include the following:

- *Limited Class Time*—Teachers believe that active student learning activities take too much class time. Using active learning activities will not allow the teacher to cover the large amount of expected content.
- *Preparation Time*—Teachers believe that active student learning activities require an excessive amount of preparation time.
- *Materials*—Teachers believe that they lack the materials or equipment to successfully implement active student learning activities.

- *Class Management*—Teachers believe that they will lose control of the class by implementing active student learning activities.
- *Student Participation*—Teachers believe that students will not participate in active student learning activities.
- *Content*—Teachers believe that the students will not be learning the required content by participating in active student learning activities.
- *Creativity*—Teachers do not have confidence in their own creativeness, resourcefulness, and imagination.
- *Adapting*—Teachers are unsure how to adapt materials or activities to accommodate for disabilities.

Teachers should not be discouraged that some students may be resistant to active student learning activities because they are accustomed to more passive learning experiences where they had to exert little or no academic effort. Realistically, teachers should expect both successes and failures when initially implementing active student learning in their classroom. Each of the obstacles listed above can be overcome with careful planning and preparation.

Active Student Learning

There are several organizational formats and instructional techniques for utilizing active student learning in the classroom. Each has their own strengths and limitations. Some will work better with some students and some objectives, whereas others will be more successful with other students and objectives. Teachers who know and understand the abilities of their students will likely be more successful with their use of active student learning activities. By trying various activities, teachers will soon realize which ones are most efficient and effective in achieving the desired outcome. This chapter section briefly describes several commonly used active student learning strategies and activities. The strategies and activities are listed in alphabetical order. They are adapted, with permission, from *Working With English Language Learners,* L.L.C. (Bergs, 2005).

- *Assignments With Choice* strategies allow students to decide how they will demonstrate that they have learned the required content. Some students may choose to demonstrate their learning by writing, others by speaking, others by drawing or illustrations, and others by building a model. For example, there may be several ways that a student could demonstrate his or her knowledge of how a bill becomes a law.

- *A–Z Taxonomy* is a language strategy. In small groups, students list the 26 letters A through Z vertically on a piece of paper. Then, based on the content, students are asked to think of terms associated with that content that start with each of the letters. For example, in the content area of "math" students might list Add, Bisect, Circle, Division, Equation, and so on. This activity can be used as both a pre- and post-instructional technique. In addition, students could be asked to define the terms or write sentences containing the term.

- *Best Choice Debate* is a strategy that asks pairs of students to first prepare either a pro or con position on a controversial content issue such as abortion or Instant Runoff Voting. A pro pair and a con pair then join to explain their position to each other and then to seek agreement on the group's best overall recommendation. The benefit of this type of strategy is that it provides speaking and listening opportunities and also practices the skill of negotiation and compromise.

- *Brainstorming* is a simple strategy to draw out numerous creative, original, imaginative, innovative, resourceful, and inventive ideas. These may be responses to open-ended questions, issues, or problems. Teachers should encourage all students to participate. In a language-diverse classroom some students may feel more comfortable responding as part of a small team of students. Since the intent of brainstorming is to solicit lots of ideas, no students should be criticized for their ideas. Sometimes it helps to set an appropriate target number of ideas when asking what lifestyle habits can cause premature death. Another strategy to use when students are having difficulties generating ideas is to reverse the statement (What things might cause premature death?).

- *Building Teamwork* is a strategy that asks small groups of students to prepare a group resume consisting of items such as hobbies, talents, travel, awards, favorite classes, schools attended, siblings, and any other information a student wishes to share. This strategy is designed to show the diversity of experiences and abilities in the class.

- *Carousel Questions* is a strategy where the teacher writes several questions about a topic (like science, social studies) on large sheets of paper posted around the room. In small groups, students rotate (for example, every 5 minutes) from one set of questions to the next. Each group of students has a different colored marker. At each station the team adds ideas/answers/responses to the paper that have not been previously listed. Share all responses when the activity concludes.

- *Case Studies* use real-life stories that describe what happened to a community, family, school, or individual to prompt students to apply their content knowledge and skill to authentic, real-world behaviors, situations, and consequences.

- *Character Maps* are ideal for some content information and concepts. Students draw a stick figure or "snowman" shaped body on their paper. Students are asked to label or generate information related to the body. For example, label the parts of the body that can be affected by cancer or the characteristics of the main character in a reading.

- *Cooperative Learning* is a strategy that involves small groups of students working together to complete a content-related project or task. Teachers using this instructional strategy often assign specific roles, duties, and tasks to specific group members. The grouping configuration may be random, voluntary, or teacher assigned. Grouping configurations should change frequently throughout the term. Teachers should appropriately group students based on the group task and student abilities.

- *Critical Explanation* asks students to think about factors or reasons that "might" explain the cause of some social issue or problem. The key word is "might." Do not use a word (such as "why") that suggests there are right or wrong answers or that has just one answer. Question triggers could include "What might explain . . . ?" or "How many reasons can you think of . . . and what are some?"

• *Discussion Web* is a teaching and learning technique where students consider a content-related problem in a small group and then regroup so each student can share his or her group's work with students who were in different task groups. This strategy works particularly well in social studies, science, health, and math. After all groups have completed their work, students decide who is A and who is B. Teachers then ask A's to remain seated and B's to stand and find a new A to be their partner. A and B then share information.

• *Field Studies* provide students with an opportunity to learn about and study content-related issues in their community. Areas of study may include health-care services, consumerism, environmental issues, political issues, biological issues, and various social issues.

• *Forced Debate* asks all students who agree with a specific issue (such as euthanasia) to sit or stand on one side of the room and all opposed on the other side. Often, hanging a sign on each side of the room helps to keep the issue clarified. After students have selected their position, switch the signs and force them to argue for the issue with which they disagree. This strategy will force the groups to consider an opposing viewpoint. To avoid predictability, vary the times when you switch, or don't switch, the signs.

• *Games* can often be used to reinforce content-related knowledge. Student-generated games can be both fun to create and play. Games can follow any common board or TV format. Games can involve matching, mysteries, group or individual competitions, solving puzzles, or can copy the format of games such as Pictionary, Jeopardy, Wheel of Fortune, Family Feud, Clue, and Scrabble. Use such things as content readings, videos, speakers, and media for the basic game information.

• *Graphic organizers* are visual representations of important content facts, concepts, and vocabulary, and how they are linked (or not linked) together. Graphic organizers can be effectively used as a focusing, primary, review, or assessment activity. Teachers should teach their students how to create and construct their own graphic organizers. Ask students to identify the main content words, ideas, sections, or content and determine relationships between and among them; determine the style/format of graphic organizer that is most appropriate for the material and purpose; use icons and pictures as well as words in their graphic organizers; and finally, when possible, use a variety of colors to represent different aspects of their graphic organizer. See Chapter 6 for more detailed information on graphic organizers.

• *Group Summarizing* is a strategy that asks students, in small groups, to summarize a content reading or observation (such as magazine article, text section, video). Younger students may need predetermined summarizing categories such as major topics, concepts, facts, and timelines. Summaries may be described in text or graphic format.

- *Group Work* allows every student the chance to speak, share ideas and information, and develop the skill of working with others. Cooperative work groups require all students to work together to complete a given task. Typical cooperative group tasks include reading articles, answering and discussing questions, sharing information, teaching subjects to other groups, creating projects, solving problems, and making decisions.

- *Guided Reciprocal Peer Questioning* is a strategy where teachers provide students with several sentence starters. Each student selects one or two sentence starters and creates a complete question based on the content information covered in class. The students don't actually have to know the answer to the question they are creating. Group students to discuss the questions each student has created. The purpose is to generate discussion. Sentence starters may include: What is . . . , Where is . . . , What can you say about . . . , Give reasons for . . . , What are the parts of . . . , What is another way . . . , What is your opinion of . . . , How can you use . . . , What is the main idea of . . . , or Why do you think . . . ?

- *"I Say" Review* is a strategy that asks pairs of students to share what they have to say about a specific content topic (such as water pollution), rather than give the correct answer to a question. This can be used as a pre- or post-strategy. Also, this strategy can be used early in the term to create a more relaxed attitude toward speaking and sharing.

- *Inside/Outside Circle* is a technique to encourage speaking about and listening to a content-related topic. Depending on the size of the class, one, two, or three circles can be used. Have 5–10 students in a circle facing outward. Match with 5–10 students in an outside circle facing a partner on the inside circle. First, for 30 seconds, outside circle students tell their partner some content information or opinion (like ways to reduce teen smoking). Next, for 10 seconds, the inside group summarizes the information received. Then the outside circle moves clockwise one or two students and repeats the information. Hint: Vary which circle moves and which circle gives information.

- *K-W-L* is a common strategy that can be productive in most content areas. The teacher, or student, makes a three-column graphic with the labels K (What I Know), W (What I Want To Find Out), and L (What I Learned). Students brainstorm what they know about a particular topic (such as How a US president is elected); next, individually or in small groups, they generate questions about what they still want to know; and finally, they read and gather information that answers their questions.

- *Logical Analogies* is a strategy where students try to find connections or analogies between a content fact or concept and a non-content fact or concept using this format: How is _____ like _____? For example: How is your nervous system like a telephone system? Ask students to generate the analogy statements. Here are some possible ending ideas: How is _____ like running for political office, running a marathon, having your first date, fighting a disease, going on a diet, building a house, going fishing, or learning a new language?

- *Minute Papers* provide students with the opportunity to summarize their content knowledge and to ask unanswered questions. Give students a minute or two in the middle or at the end of class to answer questions (in writing) such as, What was the most important thing you learned today? What can you say about . . . ? What is your opinion of . . . ? What important question remains unanswered? Use student answers to help plan upcoming lessons.

- *Music Memory* is a strategy that uses familiar ballads and songs that have passed down stories and traditions. Commercials often use familiar music and songs to promote their products. Many children remember the A, B, C song. Ask students to create a song, ballad, or jingle that will help in remembering information such as content facts, dates, formulas, rules, names, vocabulary pronunciations, or sequences.

- *Numbered Students* is a small-group (3–5 students) activity where each student in the group is given a number (1, 2, 3, 4, 5). The teacher asks a question and randomly chooses a number. The student with that number answers the question to his/her group. The teacher should select a higher-order thinking question such as "What is the healthiest food you ate yesterday? How do you know?"

- *One-Minute Club* is a review strategy designed to support the language domain of speaking. Often at the beginning of the term, the one-minute club should be reduced and referred to as the "15-Second Club." The time should then be gradually increased throughout the term. Teacher and/or student-generated content vocabulary words are placed in a "hat." Ask for student volunteers or select students to draw one out and talk about it for one minute (or 15 seconds). A pause of three seconds or more, or the use of "um" or "ah" for three seconds results in disqualification. Choose easier/familiar words at the beginning to instill confidence, especially for the special education and ELL students.

- *Outcome Sentences* are often used following videos or quest speakers. Ask students to complete a couple of statements, such as "I learned . . . ," "I was surprised . . . ," "I'm feeling . . . ," or "I would like to learn more about . . ."

- *Paired Discussions* is designed as a quick strategy in which students quickly discuss with a partner information that summarizes the class content recently presented. The activity prompt can be general or specific depending on the desired outcome or content area. Teachers should carefully structure the time by providing specific discussion time limits (such as 2 minutes).

- *Pass the Q & A* is a good strategy to emphasize important content information. The teacher suddenly announces a question and the answer. Then all students pass the question and answer along, with one student asking the question, the next answering it. Sample Question: What do the letters BMI stand for? (Answer: Body Mass Index)

- *Peer or Cross-Age Tutoring* can be done individually or in pairs. Students provide assistance to others in helping them to better understand content-related concepts. As the name implies, students assist students about the same age, younger students, older students, or students with other educational needs such as special education and English language learners.

- *Persistence Celebrations* allow the students to relax for a few minutes to celebrate the completion of a successful assignment, challenge, or task. The celebration could involve a simple stand, walk around the room, stretch, a class cheer, listening/singing to a popular song, shaking hands, giving high-fives, or letting the class determine the "unique" way (probably from a teacher or teacher-student generated list) they want to celebrate their achievements.

- *Picture Making* is similar to a graphic organizer. The teacher selects a content-related concept or piece of information that could be visually illustrated. Small groups of students create a visual illustration of the information or concept on the board or paper. When completed, groups share and discuss their illustration with other groups or the entire class.

- *Practice Test Question* is a strategy where the teacher gives the students a sample exam question for practice and then asks several students at random to report their answers to the class. Giving the students a chance to practice the type of questions they might see on the test will give them more confidence when they have to work them alone.

- *Prereading Predictions* is a strategy that allows the students, individually or in small groups, to make predictions about an upcoming reading assignment. Students should be encouraged to look at all the information including words, drawings, and photographs. For example, a teacher may select and share a few unfamiliar words from the reading and ask students to predict what the reading is about. Terms such as universe, star, telescope, planet, and gravitation might be selected for a science lesson.

- *Problem-Based Learning* is a strategy where a problem drives the learning. Students are presented with a problem prior to learning the problem-associated knowledge or skill. Students must then decide and find the information they need to solve the problem. Sample problem: What are the best ways to reduce water pollution?

- *Reaction Response* is a quick strategy where the teacher, after presenting a debatable topic, asks students to write or orally respond to a question such as "What information do you question?" or "What information is new?" Students can complete this individually or in small groups. Ask for volunteers to share their responses.

- *Role Playing* is a common strategy where the teacher asks several students to take on the roles of participants in any content-related situations being studied. This strategy can be used to demonstrate problem-solving and decision-making skills. Depending on the topic, the role-play can be spontaneous, or students might need some time to prepare. In more elaborate role-plays, students may require a few days to research and prepare for their roles. It is often important to remind students of the specific purpose of this activity. Students can role-play real or fictitious individuals from a variety of areas such as politics, medicine, arts, law, education, religion, or science.

- *Rotation Questioning* is a technique where the last student speaking calls on the next student to be the speaker. For example, student A selects and asks student B a question related to the focused content topic (such as National Parks). When student B completes his answer he calls on student C to ask a question. Student C selects and asks student D a question and so on.

- *Roundtable Writing* is a small-group writing and speaking idea-seeking strategy in which students take turns writing on a single sheet of paper. Each student says their idea aloud as they write it on the paper. Then the student passes the paper to the next student and so on.

- *Sign Language Cues* is a strategy where students are asked to generate hand or body signs for key content vocabulary. Every time you or your students say the word, use the sign as well. For example, every time the word "addition" is mentioned, the teacher and students cross their fingers to make a "plus" sign. Another good option for this activity is to teach and use "real" sign language!

- *Silence Please* involves a teacher giving directions to his or her students without speaking. These directions can be for an upcoming project, task, or assignment. As an option, ask students to respond to a question the same way—no speaking, actions only!

- *Speak or Pass* is a quick strategy where students are presented with a content question such as "Name the 13 original states." Ask each student, in turn, in a row or class section, to answer the question. Each student can answer the question or say, "I pass."

- *Statement Starters, Prompts, Triggers* help students frame and provide answers to questions that go beyond yes/no responses. Questions can be low level, such as Define . . . , Label . . . , What is . . . , and Who. . . . , or higher level, such as What is another way to . . . , Design a new . . . , Prioritize. . . . , and Why do you think . . . ?

- *Stay or Stray* is a small-group strategy where 4–6 small groups of students read, discuss, and write down information related to a different but specific component of a content issue such as AIDS. One group might read, discuss, and write about the causes of AIDS, another about group transmission, another signs and/or symptoms, another treatment, and so on. When groups are finished, one person (such as the student wearing the most red, or the student who has a May birthday, and so on) is randomly selected to *stay*. The rest of the group *strays* to the next group. The remaining individual informs the new group about the topic. After a few minutes the teacher announces which student from the new groups will stay (for example, the student who has a letter "K" in his or her name) and who will stray. As you can see, each student must pay attention to the person speaking because he or she may be the next to stay and have to share the information with the new group. A reminder poster is often helpful: "Students staying GIVE information"—"Students straying GET information." Also, a guided worksheet will often assist students.

- *Student Self–Evaluation* is a strategy where the students write a brief evaluation of their assignments, projects, and/or learning. Depending on the activity to be evaluated, it may be helpful to use sentence triggers focusing on the activity, such as problems encountered, reasons for, organization or learning process, opinions, or suggesting "another" way.

● *Student–Developed Case Studies* allow for students individually or in small groups to develop a case study of a real or fictional situation or person that presents a content-related issue or problem. Case studies can then be shared with other students or groups for reactions or solutions. Sample information might include who, what, where, when, why, or how.

● *Test Questions* allow students, individually or in small groups, to write test questions about the content covered in class. To encourage a wide range of thinking, students should write several different question formats such as multiple choice, true or false, essay, completion, or short answer. When completed, students or small groups exchange tests or groups can present their questions to the entire class. Teachers can collect the questions and use the best ones on the "real" test.

● *Think-Alouds* help students in a thinking process. For example, the teacher, in reading or describing a health-related problem, illustrates the problem-solving thinking processes out loud (verbally) for all students to hear. This strategy can be especially helpful with new vocabulary terms or sequential processes. A teacher describing the formula for determining target heart rate should say the "thinking" steps out loud such as "First I want to determine maximum heart rate; I will write down my base number 220 (male) or 224 (female). Next I will write down my age. I will then subtract my age from my base number," and so on.

● *Think-Pair-Share* is a simple strategy you can use with many content topics and in many classroom situations. Give students time to think about a content topic (such as Why was the Constitution of the United States of America developed?) for a few minutes, then turn to their neighbor for a short discussion, and then share the results with the rest of the class.

● *Thirty-Second Sound Bite for a Radio or TV Show* involves individually or in small groups students preparing a 30-second announcement designed to get listeners' attention about a content-related issue such as droughts and heat waves.

● *Three-Minute Pause* strategies are often used when the teacher is presenting some detailed or complex content. After a period of teacher-presentation time (like 10 minutes) have students pair and answer a sentence trigger such as "Discuss with your partner the main ideas of the presentation," "Discuss with your partner the functions of the vitamins described in the presentation," or "How many heart disease risk factors can you list?" After three minutes, return to presenting more health content.

● *Truth Statements* is a strategy often used at the beginning of a new content unit or topic. Ask individual or small groups of students to generate three facts they already know about a specific topic (like nuclear power plants in the US). Share the ideas/facts.

- *Value Continuums* provide students with an opportunity to physically line up according to how strongly they agree or disagree with a debatable content issue. To help students get accustomed to this strategy, it is often a good idea to first select a low-emotion issue such as "I love strawberry ice cream." Ask for student volunteers to share their viewpoint and for the other students to listen to the differing viewpoints. After a while, the teacher can move to more emotionally intense content topics such as marriage laws or drug testing.

- *Who Am I?* is a strategy to help students learn content information. Students should be divided into two or more teams. Put several content-related names on a piece of paper. Examples include:

  - I am (supply a content-related person such as William Shakespeare)
  - I am (supply a content-related event such as the Civil War)
  - I am (supply a content-related skill such as CPR)
  - I am (supply a content-related quotation such as "The fate of America cannot depend on any one man.")
  - I am (supply a content-related formula such as $a^2 + b^2 = c^2$)
  - I am (supply a content-related risk factor such as drinking and driving)
  - I am (supply a disease/condition such as Alzheimer's disease)
  - I am (supply a nutrient such as a vitamin)
  - I am (supply a content-related specialist such as an astronomer)

Teachers may be able to choose several other "Who Am I?" categories. Select students to randomly choose a piece of paper. Each team, in order, asks the student a "yes" or "no" question. The team that correctly identifies the term wins that round of the activity. Repeat with other students. As a competition option, keep track of team points.

- *Word Sorting* often helps students recognize relationships between and among content-related terms. Students are given several content-related terms and a few categories from a content unit or topic. Their task, individually or in small groups, is to group and place the terms in the categories. As an option, students are only given the terms and then asked to group the terms in ways that make sense to them—and then generate a category name for each group.

- *Write a Question* is a strategy used following a content presentation by the teacher or student. Instead of asking, "Are there any questions?" ask each student to write down two questions. The two questions may be questions the students still have about the content topic or they may be two "test" questions on the topic. Ask students to share questions with a partner, small group, or to the entire class.

Getting Started

For teachers unaccustomed to using active student learning activities, it is recommended to start with a low-risk activity. A low-risk activity is one that has a relatively short duration, utilizes partners or small groups, deals directly with the content, utilizes background information and/or experiences, and will not elicit strong disagreement or embarrassment.

An important instructional aspect to remember is not to burn out the students by repeating an activity too frequently or extending the time of an activity beyond its effectiveness.

Active student learning strategies and activities often provide students with options and opportunities to utilize their learning style preferences and abilities. You will probably notice that some of the strategies and activities will be more appealing to some learners, depending on their learning style preferences. As you read though and become familiar with the various strategies and activities, try to connect each one to one or more learning style preferences (See Chapter 4). In addition, you may think of ways to adapt the activities for a variety of disabilities and age levels.

Strategy and Activity Selection

Selecting the best teaching strategy and learning activity is often a complex task because there are many variables. A common mistake occurs when teachers select an activity because it is easy to facilitate and students enjoy it. However, teachers must remember that the purpose of a learning activity is to provide an instructional method designed to achieve one or more learning objectives. Teachers must first have a clear understanding of the students' learning objectives and then make the decision of what instructional strategy or learning activity will produce the most learning benefit to the students. Learning objectives might focus on a variety of targeted student knowledge and skills, such as seeking information, comparing, analyzing, evaluating, informing, classifying, decision making, problem solving, inquiry, self-direction, and communication.

SUMMARY

Increasing student engagement in the learning process through the selection of appropriate active learning activities has many instructional benefits. Teachers must continually consider the variety of learning styles and preferences of their students. No single instructional approach or active learning activity can be optimal for all students. New teachers should be reminded that correctly selecting student activities that engage students would generally compensate for the real or perceived obstacles that he or she may experience in the activity's implementation process.

National special education standards intrinsically require active student learning. They require learning demonstrations far beyond simple recall. Positive learning environments for students with disabilities must include a repertoire of instructional strategies that enhance critical thinking, problem solving, and performance. In addition, CEC standards promote fostering cultural understanding, safety, emotional well being, positive social interactions, and active engagement. The national special education professional standards require the demonstration of both cognitive and behavioral skills that can be most effectively achieved through active learning, which may involve activities such as repetition, practice, training, and reflection.

Walking into a classroom where students are active does not merely imply that students are learning. Quite the opposite could be true. Active learning activities often involve active students. However, there is academic purpose to their activity. The academic purpose leads directly to the knowledge and skill called for in the learning objective that targets a content's learning standard or performance indicator.

SELF-ASSESSMENT AND REFLECTION

After reading Chapter 5, please reflect on your knowledge and skill.

Self-Assessment Items

Respond to the following by answering Yes, Somewhat, or No.

I am able to

_____ 1. define and describe active student learning activities,

_____ 2. cite examples of active student learning activities that align with each of the eight learning preferences,

_____ 3. describe various strategies to implement active student learning activities,

_____ 4. describe potential strengths and limitations of many active student learning activities,

_____ 5. identify several ways to overcome common obstacles related to the implementation of active student learning activities.

Reflection

1. Which of the self-assessment items do you feel fully competent in?

2. Which of the self-assessment items do you believe need some more work, emphasis, or study time?

3. Identify two specific actions you can take to enrich and strengthen your instructional effectiveness.

6

six—seis—rau

Graphic Organizers

OBJECTIVES

1. Define and give examples of graphic organizers.

2. Give examples of how graphic organizers support teaching and learning.

3. Provide suggestions for implementing teacher-generated graphic organizers in the classroom.

4. Provide guidelines for construction of graphic organizers.

5. Describe teaching strategies for implementing student-generated graphic organizers in the classroom.

6. Suggest several examples of criteria for student-generated graphic organizers.

Suppose you were asked to describe the location of each of the 50 states of the United States—relative to each other—in written text only. One can only imagine the difficulty of this task. To write, for example in paragraph form, the location of each state relative to each of the other states would be extremely time consuming. And, from the other perspective, do you think by reading this description you could correctly assemble the arrangement of states within the United States?

Suppose you were asked, in text only, to explain the organization and location of each element on the periodic table of elements. This would be another difficult task. How accurately could you assemble the correct periodic table from this reading?

Graphic organizers can help make difficult information easier to understand. A map of the United States indicates the organization of the states. The periodic table indicates the organization of the elements.

For some students, reading a difficult section in a textbook creates the same confusion that might occur as you read the text-only version of the United States or periodic table. Seeing the visual representation of the targeted information often greatly assists learning and comprehension in all students. In some cases, the old adage may be true that a picture [graphic organizer] is worth a thousand words!

WISDOM OF PRACTICE: PICTURE THE STUDENTS!

Mr. Reid, the high school special education teacher, had several students enrolled in Mr. Hansen's high school math class. Mr. Hansen had a very diverse class: some English language learners, some on-level students, some academically talented students, and five of Mr. Reid's special education students. However, even with this diversity, Mr. Hansen chose not to differentiate his instruction. He provided identical objectives, strategies, and assessments to all students. One day, while studying United States statistical death rates, Mr. Hansen gave all of his students the following reading assignment:

> *Every day, the residents of this community experienced an average of 100 deaths. Of these 100 deaths, about 28 residents (28 percent) died from heart disease. Cancer deaths accounted for 23 deaths. Every day there were also 6 violent deaths, 4 of which were unintentional injury deaths. Of these four, two were motor vehicle deaths, one death was due to falls, and one to "all other" unintentional injury deaths. Two of the six violent deaths were other (intentional) violent deaths. In addition, 2 percent of the total daily deaths were diabetic deaths, 9 percent were respiratory deaths, and 1 percent were infant deaths. Finally, 8 percent of the daily death rates were stroke deaths.*

A couple of days later, Mr. Hansen gave all of his students a test on the reading material. Most of the students in class did poorly on the test—but not Mr. Reid's special education students. They did remarkably well! Why? When Mr. Reid saw the reading he immediately suggested that his students make graphic organizers of the reading material rather than trying to memorize the text. Students created various formats of their graphic organizers. When the students came to Mr. Hansen's test they all had an accurate visual image of the statistical death rates.

IN BRIEF: WHAT DOES THE RESEARCH SAY?

Dual-coding advocates suggest that knowledge is stored in the brain in two forms.

1. *Linguistic*—This form consists of words, phrases, and statements.

2. *Nonlinguistic or imagery*—This form consists of mental pictures.

The dual-coding theory recommends that classroom teachers use both forms—linguistic and nonlinguistic—in their instruction. The more that both forms are presented the more students are able to comprehend and recall information. It has even been shown that explicitly engaging students in the creation of nonlinguistic representations stimulates and increases activity in the brain (Gerlic & Jausovec, 1999). Unfortunately, far too many students are exposed only to the linguistic style of instruction.

A variety of teaching strategies and learning activities can support the use of non-linguistic instruction. The primary purpose of directly and purposefully including non-linguistic instruction in the classroom is to produce mental pictures of important knowledge, concepts, and skills in the minds of students.

Nonlinguistic instruction can be incorporated in the classroom in many ways. One of the more common ways is to include types of graphic organizers using various style configurations, drawings, photos, pictures, icons, signs, and symbols. The creation of physical models and utilizing other kinesthetic techniques can also enhance nonlinguistic instruction.

Solid evidence exists supporting the use of, and effectiveness of, graphic organizers. In addition to content comprehension and retention, many teachers report several student benefits including improved attitudes toward learning, improved social skills, improved thinking skills, and improved interpersonal communication skills.

Inspiration Software, Inc. (2003) materials are widely used in schools across the country to accomplish curriculum goals by incorporating and implementing the use of graphic organizers such as concept maps, idea maps, and webs.

Under the auspices of Inspiration Software, Inc., the Institute for the Advancement of Research in Education (IARE) provides educators with evidence of the instructional effectiveness of the use of graphic organizers. Using the definitions set forth by Section 9101 of the No Child Left Behind Act (NCLB) of 2001, IARE selected 29 scientifically based research studies that applied rigorous, systematic, and objective procedures to obtain reliable and valid knowledge relevant to education activities and programs.

Scientifically based research cited in the literature review demonstrates that a research base exists to support the use of graphic organizers for improving student learning and performance across grade levels, with diverse students, and in a broad range of content areas. IARE conclusions from this review include the following:

1. *Reading Comprehension*—The use of graphic organizers is effective in improving students' reading comprehension.

2. *Student Achievement*—Students using graphic organizers show achievement benefits across content areas and grade levels. Achievement benefits are also seen in students with learning disabilities.

3. *Thinking and Learning Skills*—The process of developing and using a graphic organizer enhances skills such as developing and organizing ideas, seeing relationships, and categorizing concepts.

4. *Retention*—The use of graphic organizers aids students in retention and recall of information.

5. *Cognitive Learning Theory*—The use of graphic organizers supports implementation of cognitive learning theories: dual coding theory, schema theory, and cognitive load theory.

PROFESSIONAL PRACTICE

Using visual representations to express ideas is not new. The first real evidence of language is writing. But scholars believe that writing did not appear until thousands of years after the origin of language. The earliest known written records are Sumerian word pictures made about 3500 BC and Egyptian hieroglyphics that date from about 3000 BC. Hieroglyphics is a form of writing in which picture symbols represent ideas and sounds. By about 300 BC, there were more than 6,000 symbols. Although hieroglyphics usually refers to the writing of ancient Egypt, forms of picture writing were used in other ancient cultures as well, notably by the Hittites, who lived in the region that is now Turkey, and by the Maya and Aztec Indians of Central America (Cardona, 2005).

Graphic Organizers

Graphic organizers, in the context of classroom instruction, are visual representations of information, facts, concepts, and skills, and how these items are (or may be) linked, or not linked, together. Graphic organizers are sometimes called mind maps, webs, or visual organizers. Graphic organizers are adaptable to virtually all content areas, grade levels, and student ability levels. They can be especially helpful with special education students and English language learners. Gifted and talented students often enjoy the challenge of transposing complex information into visual representations. In addition, graphic organizers can be effectively used during many phases of instruction.

Graphic organizers can be used in the following ways:

1. At the beginning of a unit or lesson as a way to determine and/or activate prior knowledge.

2. During the main course of instruction to achieve both content objectives and language objectives.

3. At the end of a unit or lesson for student assessment and evaluation purposes.

Graphic organizers have the ability to support most academic disciplines and many content and topic areas. The various styles of graphic organizers are readily available to support common patterns of information. These patterns include

- sequence,
- descriptive,
- cause-effect,
- compare-contrast,
- hierarchical,

- chronological,
- conceptual, and
- circular.

One of the most recognizable and commonly used graphic organizers is the Venn diagram, which uses two or more overlapping circles. A simple two-circle Venn diagram (Figure 6.1) is often used to compare (different and similar) characteristics of two items or ideas. For example, students may be asked to compare two diseases such as Lyme disease and West Nile virus.

Figure 6.1 Two-Circle Venn Diagram

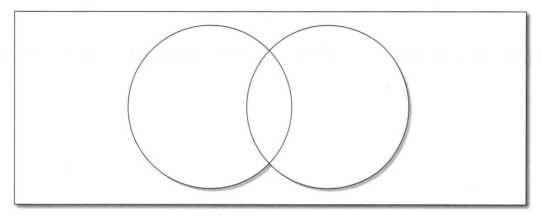

To increase rigor, a teacher might add a third circle (Figure 6.2) and add another disease such as avian influenza.

Figure 6.2 Three-Circle Venn Diagram

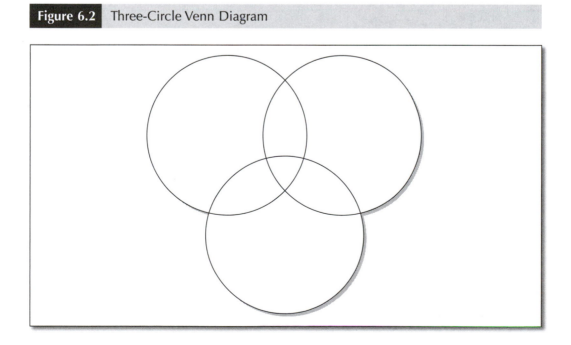

Another commonly used graphic organizer is the concept or descriptive map (Figure 6.3). This graphic organizer pattern is commonly used to conceptualize a person (like Abraham Lincoln), place (Washington DC), or thing (bird). This pattern might also be used to conceptualize a multiple-meaning word (such as scale).

Figure 6.3 Descriptive Map

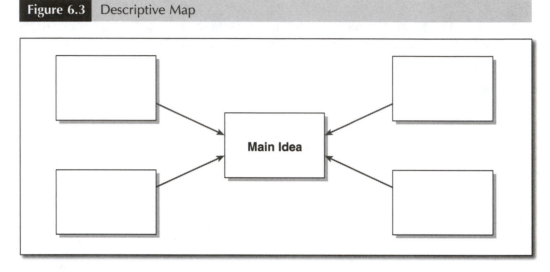

When teachers want their student to learn a specific order or sequence, they often select a sequence pattern graphic organizer (Figure 6.4) to facilitate student learning. Sequence charts are often used to highlight important historical events, specific steps in a procedure (such as CPR), or to conceptualize the transmission of a communicable disease from its source to a susceptible host. Teachers often use sequence charts to help students follow specified steps to completing a learning assignment.

Figure 6.4 Sequence Chart

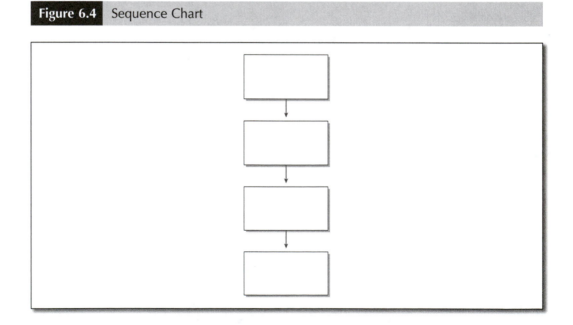

A T-Chart (Figure 6.5) is another frequently used graphic organizer. The simple pattern makes it easy for students to understand and use.

Figure 6.5 T-Chart

A Four-Cell T-Chart allows students to examine two aspects of an issue or topic. Examples of the aspects, labeled on each side of the T-Chart, include pros and cons, advantages and disadvantages, or facts and opinions. T-Charts with blank cells (Figure 6.6) may be helpful for some students.

Figure 6.6 Four-Cell T-Chart

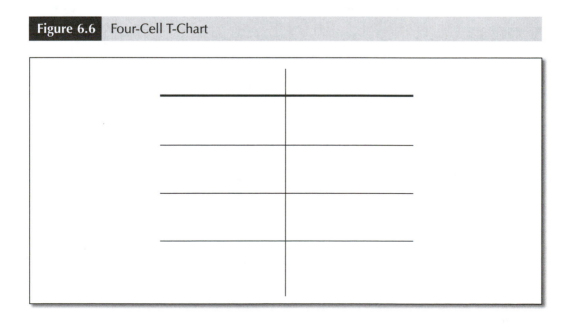

Graphic Organizer Formats and Uses

There are literally dozens of formats, layouts, designs, and styles of graphic organizers. However, each one is typically best suited to describe and organize a specific type of information.

James Bellanca (2007) offers these ideas and suggestions for selecting the appropriate graphic organizer to illustrate specific information.

1. A Concept (Figure 6.7) or Web Map (Figure 6.8) works well for mapping generic information, but particularly well for activating and mapping prior knowledge, brainstorming ideas, and gathering information from print or visual materials.

Figure 6.7 Concept Map

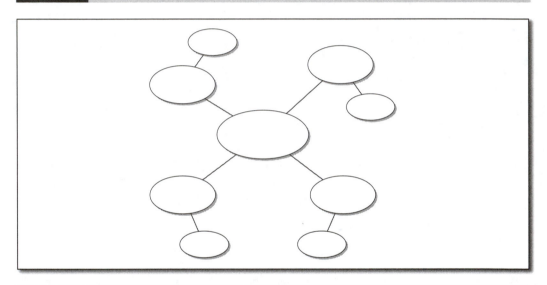

Figure 6.8 Web Map

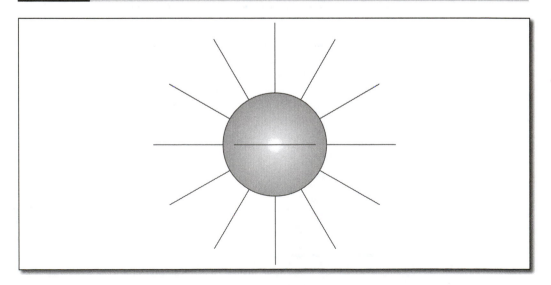

2. When the information relating to a main idea or theme does not fit into a hierarchy, a Spider Map (Figure 6.9) can help with organization. The Spider Map is often used to connect specific details to a main concept or idea such as in a story, article, or discussion.

Figure 6.9 Spider Map

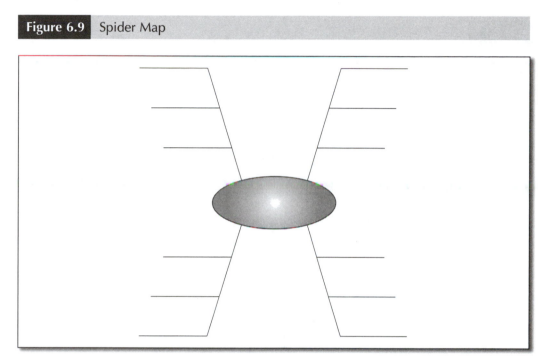

3. When information contains cause and effect problems and possible solutions, a Fishbone (Figure 6.10) can be useful for organizing and visualizing various influences on specific events. Additional rectangles can be easily added to the Fishbone Map if multiple effects and/or solutions are generated.

Figure 6.10 Fishbone Map

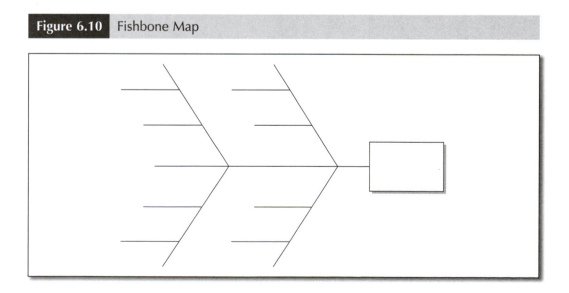

4. A Decision-Making Map (Figure 6.11) helps students in the decision-making process or to compare different solutions to a problem. The map below illustrates the space for four possible alternatives to the question or problem and space for the positives (+) and negatives (−) of each alternative.

Figure 6.11 Decision-Making Map

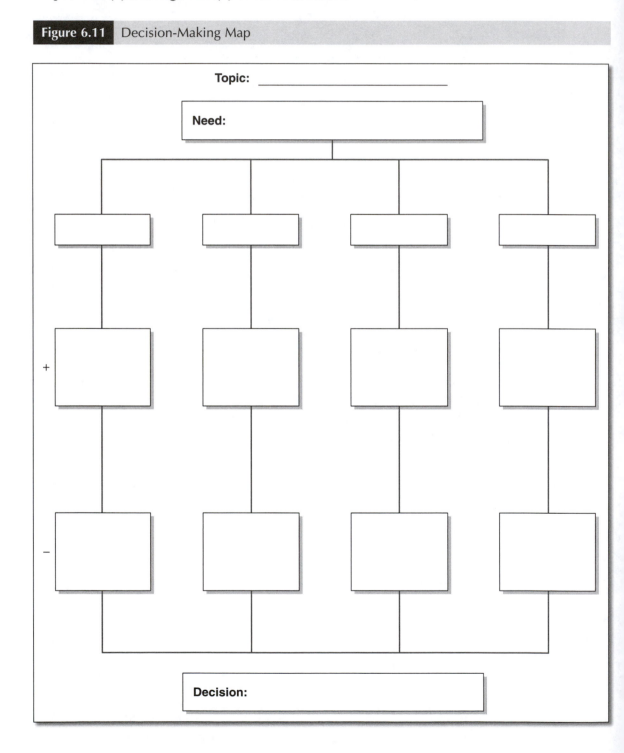

5. Continuum Maps (Figure 6.12) are an effective way of organizing information along a dimension such as less to more, low to high, and few to many. A continuum map may also be used to illustrate a time line of, for example, important dates in the history of an important event or topic.

Figure 6.12	Continuum Map

Example: Continuum Map

├--┤
Low   High

6. A Cycle Map (Figure 6.13) is useful for organizing information that is circular or cyclical, with no absolute beginning or ending.

Figure 6.13	Cycle Map

7. A Body Map (Figure 6.14) is one instructional option when dealing with various health-related issues such as how or where various diseases affect the body, basic anatomy, or the effects of hypothermia.

Figure 6.14 Body Map

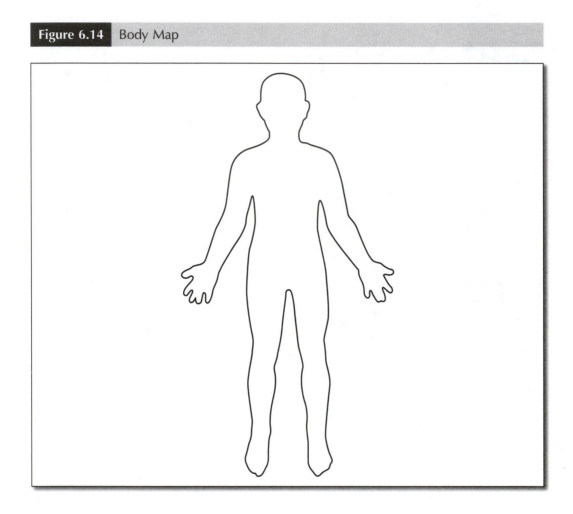

Teacher-Generated Graphic Organizers

Teacher generated graphic organizers are a good way to introduce and integrate graphic organizers into classroom instruction.

Some suggestions on how to introduce and use graphic organizers in the classroom include the following:

1. Explain the purpose and benefits of using graphic organizers to the students. This may include:
   o the importance of organizing information;
   o how using a visual organizer can aid retention, comprehension, and recall.

2. Introduce a specific graphic organizer.

   o Describe its purpose such as cause and effect, compare and contrast, a continuum, sequence of events, hierarchical, descriptive, or thematic.

   o Describe its form, such as two intersecting circles, a center circle with straight lines extending from it, boxes connected by arrows, or the specific shape of an object such as an house, sea shell, clock, pie, or human body.

3. Explain and model how to use the selected organizer with old and/or new information.

4. Let students, individually or in pairs, apply the graphic organizer to old and/or new information.

5. Have students reflect on what they liked about using graphic organizers and how they might adapt them for use in other contexts.

6. Provide multiple opportunities for the students to practice using graphic organizers.

7. Eventually and gradually, encourage students to create and construct their own graphic organizers.

Construction of Graphic Organizers

Teachers and students can effectively and creatively develop graphic organizers. However, there are a few general guidelines. These include the following:

1. *Identify* the main ideas, sections, or content.

2. *Cluster* or group words and ideas that are related.

3. *Determine relationships* (cause and effect, sequential, chronological).

4. *Determine the type* of graphic organizer that is most appropriate for the material and purpose.

5. *Arrange ideas* and draw connecting lines. Lines can be straight, curved, or wiggly to convey the message.

6. Remember, there are *many ways* to visually represent ideas; don't be afraid to change the style or format of the graphic organizer.

7. Use *icons, photos, drawings, and pictures,* as well as words, in your graphic organizer.

8. When possible, *use a variety of colors* to represent different aspects of the graphic organizer.

Student-Created Graphic Organizers

Many teachers fail to realize that one of the important instructional benefits of graphic organizers is when students are challenged to create their own. Often times, several students working independently, will create and organize the identical content information in entirely different ways. Even so, each of these ways may characterize an accurate representation of the information. For example, suppose the teacher asks students to make a visual representation of the athletic sports offered at their school. As you might guess, some students might organize the sports by gender, some by season, some by the degree of physical contact, and others by participation fees. And all could be entirely accurate!

Some teachers give graphic organizer assignments to students (with a partner or in small groups) where a traditional graphic organizer pattern, such as a Venn diagram or pie chart *cannot* be used. Teachers are often amazed at the students' imagination, creativity, and inventiveness. Depending on the topic, students might select as their pattern such things as airplanes, a US state shape, cars, flowers, athletic equipment, musical notes, or animals.

However, before expecting students to create graphic organizers independently, teachers should consider these suggestions:

1. Clearly *demonstrate* the use of and construction of graphic organizers.

2. Give students *partially constructed* graphic organizers for practice.

3. Remember to *scaffold* instruction: direct instruction > modeling > practice > student independence.

4. Use *caution* when showing examples of graphic organizers. Showing examples could stymie the students' creativity.

One way to begin is to think about an upcoming topic and associated information that your students will be reading, hearing, writing, or seeing. Then develop a student assignment (individual, partner, or small group) information sheet that describes their task to create a graphic organizer linking the information identified above. It's often a good idea to make a quick sketch of several possible ways the students' graphic organizers might look. By having a couple of formats in mind, the teacher will be able to offer some concrete suggestions to struggling students.

As mentioned previously, having students create their own graphic organizers has many academic teaching and learning advantages. One way to increase the students' accountability and learning is by preparing a checklist or rubric for the students to follow.

Some suggested criteria for student-generated graphic organizers include the following:

1. The information is accurate.

2. The information is complete.

3. The information is clear (easy to interpret).

4. The information is neat and presentable.

5. The vocabulary is appropriate.

6. The student can verbally explain his/her graphic organizer to others.

7. The completion timelines are followed.

8. The student's name is on the graphic organizer.

9. The use of multiple colors enhances the graphic organizers.

10. The use of icons, photos, pictures, and/or drawings enhances the graphic organizers.

11. The format and style is supportive of the information.

Graphic Organizers: A Sample Activity

Suppose a teacher was preparing to teach a United States geography lesson and wanted to give a pretest to determine prior knowledge and student readiness.

The teacher could give these directions to the students working independently or in pairs—after making sure that each had paper and pencil.

1. Draw, from memory, an outline map of the continental United States and add Alaska and Hawaii.

2. Draw one horizontal line (east to west) that separates the continental United States into two sections—a northern section and a southern section.

3. Draw three vertical lines (north to south) that separate the United States into four sections—one western section, two middle sections, and one eastern section.

4. You now have a total of eight sections on your map.

5. In the time given (for instance, 5 minutes), name as many states as you can by putting the state's name in the correct United States section.

During this activity, the teacher can roam throughout the classroom to observe the degree to which the students are able to adequately complete their task. Used as a pretest, this observation may well provide the teacher with enough data to determine an appropriate instructional starting point.

Graphic Organizers and Classroom Management

Many teachers report that using both teacher-generated and student-generated graphic organizers makes a positive and noticeable difference in classroom and behavior management. Lesson design and classroom management are closely related. Teachers successful in classroom management are excellent planners and are well prepared in the use of time and materials. They are able to maximize student learning in the given amount of time. This is especially true when using graphic organizers, since they may require various materials such as paper, markers, rulers, and magazines. However, the use of a well-planned graphic organizer lesson can often lead to active and engaged students resulting in improved learning.

There are very few, if any, instructional strategies that are consistently effective and productive with all students all of the time. However, many teachers report that the use of graphic organizers is the one instructional strategy that is time and again the most useful in helping students achieve academic success.

Using the examples in this chapter as a starting point will provide teachers and students with effective ways to visually organize and represent a wide variety of content facts, concepts, and skills.

SUMMARY

Graphic organizers are an effective way to help students understand important facts, concepts, and skills. There are literally dozens of formats that can be selected to create a graphic organizer. This chapter has illustrated only a few formats and patterns. Many students like to create their own "unique" format or a "variation" to a common format. Graphic organizers can be used effectively in whole-class instruction as well as in small-group, partner, and individual instruction.

Providing instruction to students on ways to construct and use graphic organizers often presents a path to higher student learning and academic achievement.

SELF-ASSESSMENT AND REFLECTION

After reading Chapter 6, please reflect on your knowledge and skill.

Self-Assessment Items

Respond to the following by answering Yes, Somewhat, or No.

I am able to:

_____ 1. Define and give examples of graphic organizers,

_____ 2. Give examples of how graphic organizers support teaching and learning,

_____ 3. Provide suggestions for implementing teacher-generated graphic organizers in the classroom,

_____ 4. Provide guidelines for construction of graphic organizers,

_____ 5. Describe teaching strategies for implementing student-generated graphic organizers in the classroom,

_____ 6. Suggest several examples of criteria for student-generated graphic organizers.

Reflection

1. Which of the self-assessment items do you feel fully competent in?

2. Which of the self-assessment items do you believe you need some more work, emphasis, or study time for?

3. Identify two specific actions you can take to enrich and strengthen your instructional effectiveness.

seven—siete—xya

Incorporating Technology

7

1. Identify legal and practical reasons to incorporate technology.

2. Define and give examples of assistive technology.

3. Integrate assistive technology that supports student learning.

4. Explain universal design for learning.

5. Incorporate universal design for learning in instructional practice.

6. Identify technology that is used to motivate learners.

Technology provides teachers the opportunity to utilize a variety of instructional presentation and assessment options, coordinate data collection, maintain student records, research content or disability-specific information, and more readily communicate with other professionals, students, and parents. For students with disabilities, technology supports independence and provides opportunities to engage with peers in academics and extracurricular activities. Tools used by teachers and students to gather, hold, and manipulate data are getting faster, smaller, and smarter. Technology to support learning is becoming more mainstream, and individuals are getting more creative in using resources that accompany the digital age.

In Chapter 7 the reader will learn how technology can be utilized to increase professional productivity and enhance instruction. Effective practices in selecting Assistive Technology (AT) and implementing universal design for learning (UDL) will be discussed. Suggestions for using technology to ensure compliance and engage students are included.

WISDOM OF PRACTICE:
EMMALEE JONES—DIGITAL IMMIGRANT OR NATIVE?

Emmalee Jones was exasperated. When she accepted the job as a special education teacher for students with learning disabilities at Riverdale Junction High School she was told there were computers for the students to use in her resource room. When she arrived, the students in first hour told her the last teacher always let them sit at her desk and use her computer "to do e-mail and research because it had Internet and was better." Miss Jones met with the principal, Mr. Talbutt, to inquire about upgrading the student computers. He told her the budget didn't include upgrades this year, and furthermore, the students had abused Internet privileges last year.

Ending One: That night Emmalee (the digital immigrant) thought about her discussion with Mr. Talbutt. She would create a policy that restricted students from using the teacher's computer. However, to compensate for that, she would allow students to go use computers in the library.

Ending Two: That night Emmalee (the digital native) thought about her discussion with Mr. Talbutt. She had to be resourceful and came up with a plan quickly! By morning, Emmalee had formulated a technology plan that included student responsibility, collaboration with general education teachers, and partnering with the business community. She was excited to talk to Mr. Talbutt.

Challenges and opportunities are inherent in the use of technology. Along with the legal basis for considering and using technology in academic settings, special education teachers like Emmalee Jones can use creative solutions to support and benefit the educational needs of students with disabilities. This chapter provides ideas to effectively incorporate technology that enhances professional efficacy and instruction.

IN BRIEF: WHAT DOES THE RESEARCH SAY?

Technology is considered by some to be an innovation in education. The definition of technology is broad. In general, technology includes equipment, tools, devices, electronic hardware, software, cyberspace, and systems' infrastructures. Technology can be highly complex or relatively simple. Technology may be needed for medical, orthopedic, or academic purposes. Assessment using technology has created better options for ensuring access and reliability (Salend, 2009). Team decisions provide for the use of technology as part of the instructional environment.

Knowledge and use of technology divides individuals into two groups sometimes called digital immigrants and digital natives (Prensky, 2001). The immigrant may be less savvy in knowing what technology exists and what it can do, but may offer creative and frugal ideas to solve technology situations. Digital natives tend to be risk-takers in trying out new technologies. The native recognizes the power of computers and other personal communication devices and is willing to push technology to extremes. The digital native who has grown up with multitasking in a technology rich, globally connected, information-explosive age may be less able to comprehend the advantages of a low-tech environment for some students and families.

Contemporary use of technology promotes instructional methods to engage learners and enhance learning among all students (Castellani & Jeffs, 2001). More emphasis is being placed on collecting empirical evidence to understand the role of technology in closing the achievement gap for students with disabilities and other subgroups. One such study by Johns Hopkins University Center for Technology in Education used GLOBE Tech to incorporate the principles of cooperative learning (Mainzer, Castellani, Lowry, & Nunn, 2006). This framework for instruction involves mixed-ability groups, peer-assisted learning, and a variety of tools in an effort to study the academic impact of technology in general education classrooms where students with disabilities are included.

Diverse students benefit from the increased use of digital communication and the use of technology to engage them in the learning process. English Language Acquisition Technology (ELAT) has been found to be a promising practice for improving language acquisition and academic success for ELL students with learning disabilities (Lowdermilk, Fielding, Mendoza, Garcia de Alba, & Simpson, 2008). "Cool" technology that students help select is more likely to be used by a student (Parette, Wojcik, Peterson-Karlan, & Hourcade, 2005). The use of technology by students can better prepare them for the future and can give them skills they will need to be independent (Hasselbring & Glaser, 2000; Stodden, Galloway, & Stodden, 2003). Strong support for incorporating technology also comes from legislation.

No Child Left Behind

No Child Left Behind (NCLB) legislation highlights technology. Part D, a section of the NCLB Act (2001) called Enhancing Education Through Technology, also known as E2T2, notes the following goal:

> To assist every student in crossing the digital divide by ensuring that every student is technologically literate by the time the student finishes the eighth grade, regardless of the student's race, ethnicity, gender, family income, geographic location, or disability. (NCLB, 2001).

Individuals With Disabilities Education Improvement Act

In addition, the Individuals with Disabilities Education Improvement Act (IDEIA) of 2004 requires that the assistive technology needs of all students be considered in the IEP planning process (PL105–17, Section 1414 (d)(3)(B)(v)). As with other areas of programming in special education, it is not necessary to provide the most expensive piece of technology. However, consideration must be given to "if" and "which" assistive technology will benefit the educational needs of the student.

Both NCLB and IDEIA have directed educators to consider technology as an integral component of education. Teachers who are technologically proficient see a connection between technology and curriculum, are aware of the school's culture in organizing and using technology, and are more successful in integrating the use of technology (Zhao, Pugh, Sheldon, & Byers, 2002). Today, technology standards are incorporated in most professional content areas.

Technology Standards

The International Society for Technology and Education (ISTE) has created standards to ensure teachers are knowledgeable of and able to demonstrate skills in technology. The National Education Technology Standards—Teacher (NETS—T) are organized around five themes designed to support productivity in professional practice, to enhance teaching and learning environments—including inspiring creativity—and to address digital experiences that model social and human issues related to work, citizenship, responsibility, and leadership. The standards are available at http://www.iste.org/Content/NavigationMenu/ NETS/ForTeachers/2008Standards/NETS_for_Teachers_ 2008.htm.

National Educational Technology Standards—Students (NETS—S) also exist. The ISTE student standards address six areas including knowing the basics of how to use technology, using technology for creative purposes, communication, research, critical thinking, and demonstrating digital responsibility. Read more about NETS-S at http://www.iste.org/Content/NavigationMenu/NETS/ForStudents/2007Standards/ NETS_for_Students_2007.htm.

PROFESSIONAL PRACTICE

The educational landscape has changed dramatically since the mid-seventies when special education laws were enacted. More than ever, computers and other technological innovations are relied upon as professional and academic tools.

Incorporating Technology: Practical and Painless Suggestions

The digital divide is real. Access to technology may be restricted by location, interest, or expense associated with owning technology. Blending innovation and reality is necessary as a special educator to keep pace with job responsibilities.

Coordinating Due Process and Communication

Special education teachers incorporate technology as part of their role and responsibility in their career.

1. Electronic Templates for Legal Forms

Many local school districts have electronic due process forms designed to meet all state and federal requirements for special education. Using templates for IEPs, assessment reports, meeting notices, or recording parent contacts increases the productivity of special education teachers and ensures compliance by having all legal components built into the document. It has been estimated that average special education teachers spend as much as twenty percent of their time (Edds, 2002), or from one-half to one-and-a-half days a week (Goldstein, 2003) on paperwork. Computer-assisted IEP development software (CAIDS) is more user friendly and can save time (Serfass & Peterson, 2007).

Templates and spreadsheets promote data collection and accountability. Rather than hand-counting data, well-designed systems can quickly retrieve the number of students identified in federal disability categories, placements, numbers of referrals, types of interventions, demographics, grades, school attendance, achievement scores, behavioral infractions, and other program information.

Technology supports confidentiality of information when the data is treated confidentially. In order to use electronic special education templates, most districts require training, authorization, and regular updates as changes in forms or legal requirements occur. Security and safety are ensured by the care you take in entering passwords and sending information.

2. E-mail Communication

Given the various people who are involved in the special education process, e-mail serves as a communication tool to readily share information. Language, tone of voice, timing, and length of the communication all impact the message received. Consider the following points:

- Some messages are better off not being sent by e-mail. Rethink a response before sending comments in a moment of frustration or anger. Enforce "lag time" for yourself before responding. Communicate sensitive information in person.
- Ask if there is a policy about using student names or identification numbers in e-mails.
- Ask families if they have access to a home computer before sending messages electronically.
- When using e-mail to communicate with families or general educators, find out when (or if) they check e-mail.
- E-mail messages can provide a paper trail to document compliance when there are disputes.

Promoting Productivity

It's helpful to consider technology as an area for professional development. Attend building or district training that introduces new software, technical procedures, or equipment. Ask veteran teachers about shortcuts they use when completing due process templates. Some practical suggestions include the following:

- Use the SAVE function often when writing assessment reports or IEPs.
- Type everything on a Word document first, then cut and paste it into the template.
- Proofread to avoid embarrassing mistakes such as finding another student's name in a document that was cut and pasted.
- Start early when writing IEPs and other required reports.
- Send reminders to other team members who are adding to the report.
- Use an e-mail calendar to set up appointments and IEP meetings.
- Don't procrastinate. District computer systems are known to fail during periods of heavy use.
- Memorize the phone number of the instructional technology HELP desk.
- Use drop-down functions to select objectives for IEPs.
- Fill out the contact log daily.
- Use district attendance and grading software.

Trouble Shooting and Maintaining Equipment

Find out what technological support is provided. Know who has the responsibility for maintenance and trouble shooting in order to keep equipment repaired and in working order. Introduce yourself to that person. Some important questions to ask are as follows:

1. Is the same person responsible for maintenance of student and staff computers and software?

2. Who is the contact individual for assistance with other equipment such as televisions, VCRs or DVDs, CD or cassette players, overhead projectors, movie cameras, electronic whiteboards, or LCD projectors?

3. Is there an assistive technology team? Who are the members?

4. Who notifies the occupational therapist, physical therapist, hearing or vision teacher when student equipment fails?

Write the names and contact information of technology support staff in a prominent place in order to contact the right person when concerns arise.

Identifying Responsibilities and Safety Issues

For student equipment, software, or devices designed for individual use, know the contact person, phone number, e-mail address, and product Web site should questions arise. Update these regularly. Organize a three-ring binder with copies of signed contracts and user guides. Keep the salesperson's business card inserted in a plastic page protector with the maintenance agreement. Document the schedule of routine procedures to maintain proper working order.

Student safety in using equipment should be taken seriously. Electric devices and their location should be checked regularly. Avoid overloading outlets and keep cords away from high-traffic areas. Use ground fault interrupters as another precaution.

Determine who is responsible for replacing batteries in equipment. As a special educator, the responsibility for replacing hearing-aid batteries may be yours, the speech language therapist's, or the teacher's for students with hearing impairments. Have extra batteries available to avoid losing instruction time.

Budgeting for Equipment

It is difficult to anticipate all expenses associated with technology. Expenditures for items listed on IEPs are incurred by districts or addressed through third-party billing of a parent's insurance. Districts will purchase and upgrade student and teacher computers, phone and Internet services, and software critical for record keeping and educational purposes. Some instructional equipment is the responsibility of the special education department. This might include hand-held devices such as electronic spelling devices or calculators used for learning. Costs related to daily wear and tear such as replacement of batteries or headphones should be itemized on annual budget requests.

Storing Equipment

The location of equipment should be consistent with where it will be used, who will be using it, and who is responsible for it. If the special educator attaches and removes the communication device to and from the student's wheelchair daily, the equipment should be housed in the special education room, preferably in a storage cabinet that can be locked. Keep the key in a location known by at least one other person who can assist the student in your absence. When selecting a storage location, the room temperature should be controlled to avoid damage from heat, humidity, and cold.

Establishing Policies and Practices

Classroom phones, cell phones, personal music players and ear buds, tablet computers, and wireless communication devices are becoming more common and available. Computers, personal communication devices, Web sites, or software for data collection are effective and enhance efficiency, but you should know the policies regarding staff and student use. Follow district technology guidelines listed in staff and student handbooks.

Some districts allow teachers to take school laptops home to complete entering data on evaluation summaries or IEPs. Ask if this is permissible.

Explain school policies to students or establish fair-use practices for students where there are none. For example, texting on a cell phone during a test is considered unauthorized communication and may be treated as cheating.

Teachers have a responsibility to help children understand online safety issues and acceptable use of technology. Many districts have students sign an "Acceptable Use Agreement." Confidentiality and security are primary concerns when using technology. As in any professional situation, technology must be used in ways that guarantee student privacy and safety. Stay alert to red flags. Cyberbullying, or misuse of Facebook, MySpace, or other social networks often spills over into school hallways. The use of Internet is a privilege and a responsibility. "No tolerance policies" are in place for those who mismanage computer time or log on to inappropriate Web sites. Schools have safety nets that restrict some cyber locations, but periodically browse through the Web site history to be aware of what students are accessing.

Wheelchairs, digital voice synthesizers, and other technology needed by some students with disabilities can by highly sensitive and very expensive. Teach peers to keep hands off of the equipment needed by classmates.

Assistive Technology to Support Students

As a special educator it will be necessary to assess and prepare students with disabilities for learning opportunities and environments where they will use technology. The Individuals with Disabilities Education Act (IDEA, 1997) mandates that assistive technology be considered as part of the IEP process. If assistive technology is determined to be necessary for the student to benefit from education and to have access to the general curriculum, then the IEP must specify the devices and services needed.

Most districts have a policy that must be followed when conducting an assistive technology evaluation or writing the need for equipment into an IEP. *Before* recommending a piece of equipment, know the policy.

Defining Assistive Technology

According to IDEA (1997), an assistive technology device is "any item, piece of equipment, or product system whether acquired commercially off the shelf, modified, or customized that is used to increase, maintain, or improve the functional capability of a child with a disability" (34 C.F.R. 300.5, p. 11). Assistive technology services ensure the evaluation of a child for assistive technology, purchasing, leasing, selecting, designing, fitting, customizing, adapting, applying, maintaining, repairing, replacing, coordinating and using other therapies with the assistive technology, and providing technical assistance to the child, family and other professionals providing education (IDEA, 1997, 34 C.F.R. 300.5, p. 11).

Levels of Assistive Technology

Students with disabilities benefit by being able to use calculators, computers, sticky notes, highlighters, soft-grip pens, and software that provide immediate feedback. These are assistive tools that support academic achievement.

Assistive technology does not have to be high-end equipment if a retrofitted or simple device can accomplish the same purpose. It is important to begin with the least expensive or complicated tool in order to achieve the greatest academic gain when considering what to use with students. Assistive technology is described on a range of complexity from low to high, as noted in Table 7.1.

Table 7.1	Assistive Technology in the Classroom		
Academic Skills	**Low Technology**	**Mid Technology**	**High Technology**
Math calculation	Abacus	Handheld calculator	Computer
Note-taking	Peer taking notes	Recording lectures on a cassette player	Text to speech software
Organizing information	Highlighting marker	Highlight tape	Computer software that highlights text
Writing	Pencil with an eraser	Handheld electronic speller	Predictive writing software
Orthopedic independence for leisure skills	Paraprofessional turns the radio on and off	Handheld switch activates the radio	Radio is voice activated

When writing an IEP, special education teams must determine if AT is needed. Decisions must be related to the individual student goals, classroom academic expectations, setting, and technology options.

Making Assistive Technology Decisions

Assistive technology consideration is a recurring special education process. Teams should review AT options during the following times:

1. When the student is referred

2. During the evaluation process

3. In the development of an IEP

4. During the implementation of service

5. As a part of progress monitoring

Common errors for teams to avoid include the following:

- Assistive technology is considered only for students with severe disabilities.
  - Reality: All students on an IEP should be part of an AT consideration process.

- The IEP team is missing a member who is knowledgeable about assistive technology.
  - o Reality: An occupational therapist or other district staff may be designated to serve as a contact person for AT consideration at IEP meetings.
- Teams fail to consider access to the general education curriculum when determining the need for assistive technology.
  - o Reality: The team should consider all settings when selecting AT.
- Individualized goals and objectives are not matched with assistive technology needs.
  - o Reality: Goals and objectives should serve as a foundation for the AT decision.

Steps in Making Assistive Technology Decisions

The steps in Table 7.2 can be used in determining the student's assistive technology needs. Sample responses are provided. Focus on the student's goal to establish a clear plan and remain learner centered. Involve the IEP team in the discussion.

It is recommended the team implement the AT choice on a trial basis. Agree to revisit the decision after several weeks. During that time, gather data on student achievement. If the student is making progress, finalize the assistive technology decision as part of the IEP.

A well-known AT decision-making model is SETT, developed by Joy Zabala (October, 1995). For a description, see http://www.edtechpolicy.org/SETTBRIEFINTRO.pdf.

Determining Financial Responsibility

Once a team determines that AT is required for the child to benefit from education, the school district must assume financial responsibility for the purchase of devices and services. Unknowingly, some new teachers obligate districts to buy expensive equipment because the teachers don't know the AT policy. There are options to schools bearing the cost of assistive technology, including the following:

- The cost of the device or service is covered by third-party benefits.
- The cost is covered by insurance, and parents agree to use such coverage to pay the cost.
- The cost is covered by a donation to the school district.
- Funding is sought externally from other sources.

Exploring any of the above options should not delay providing the student with the assistive technology or service. As a requirement of IDEA, students are guaranteed a free, appropriate public education (FAPE). In short, AT is provided at no cost to parents. Assistive technology teams are adept at providing options and knowing policies.

Incorporating Universal Design for Learning

Since 1984, the Center for Applied Special Technology (CAST) has worked to create educational experiences that eliminate boundaries for individuals with disabilities.

Table 7.2 Steps in Assistive Technology Decisions

Step 1: The Student Goal	Team Responses	Comments
What is the learning goal from the IEP?	The student will pass English.	
What makes the learning goal difficult or impossible?	The student has no fine motor skills and is unable to write legibly due to TBI.	
What strengths and abilities does the student bring to the classroom?	The student is motivated. The student has lots of friends.	
What task must we address?	The student needs to meet writing requirements (take notes, essay tests, research papers, daily quizzes).	
Step 2: Classroom and Instruction	**Team Responses**	
What is the room arrangement and teaching style?	Students sit in rows while the teacher lectures.	
What support is available to the student and teacher?	Special education teacher serves as a consultant.	
What materials and equipment are commonly used?	Students use computers.	
Are there technological, physical or instructional access issues?	Students sit in rows. Computers are behind teacher's desk.	Can the computers be moved?
Are there attitudes or expectations of staff, family, or others to consider?	Everyone has high expectations.	

(Continued)

Table 7.2 (Continued)

Step 3: Information Alignment	Team Responses	
Analyze: How does student goal align with task and instruction?	Student has ability and desire but needs AT support.	
Brainstorm: What low-, mid-, or high-tech options could support student achievement?	*Low tech.* The student will not be required to take notes. Instead, he will go to the special education classroom after lectures to dictate reflections to the education assistant. *Mid tech.* A peer will take notes and make copies. The student will record reflections on a tape recorder. *High tech.* The student will use a computer and voice-activated predictive writing software during class lectures.	
Consider: Will the student be able to make reasonable progress toward educational goals without assistive technology devices and services?	No	
Decide: Which one of the brainstormed assistive technology options is best?	High Tech	Need to view and buy voice-activated software and earbuds

Universal design for learning evolved as an idea aimed at removing barriers for individuals with disabilities. Architects originally took the concept of universal design and began creating environments that welcomed and met the needs of individuals whose vision, mobility, or access might have been restricted.

Defining UDL

The Assistive Technology Act of 1998 defined UDL as "a philosophy or concept for designing and delivering products and services." (PL 105-394, USC 2432, ss1 (b) (3)). UDL was further defined in the Higher Education Opportunity Act (2008) as a scientifically valid framework for guiding educational practice that

(A) Provides flexibility in the ways information is presented, in the ways students respond or demonstrate knowledge and skills, and in the ways students are engaged; and

(B) Reduces barriers in instruction, provides appropriate accommodations, supports, and challenges and maintains high-achievement expectations for all students, including students with disabilities and students who are limited English proficient. (Higher Education Opportunity Act, 2008, PL110-135, section 24 A B, p.12).

Further clarification made by CAST notes that UDL is "a framework that can help you turn challenges posed by high standards and increasing learner diversity into opportunities to maximize learning for every student" (CAST, 2010). The IDEA requires all students with disabilities to have access to curriculum consistent with their peers. Research conducted by CAST has resulted in more opportunities for all students to have access to general education curriculum by building on the power of digital technology.

Using UDL in Classrooms

Universal design for learning incorporates the concept of differentiation. When combined with assistive technology, differentiation reinforces opportunities for students with disabilities to achieve. Special and general education teachers can work together in setting goals, choosing or creating flexible materials and media, and assessing students accurately. This enhances student learning by providing:

1. multiple means to acquire information,

2. alternative processes for demonstrating knowledge,

3. motivation.

   (National Center on Universal Design for Learning, 2009)

How does the student acquire information?

When considering universal design or assistive technology, identify how information is displayed and whether the student's needs are auditory, visual, or physical. Look for technology that supports knowledge with:

- Pictures or other nonlinguistic representations (such as charts, timelines),
- Content-specific vocabulary and symbols,
- Age-appropriate language and sentence structure,
- Support for decoding text or math problems,
- Bilingual considerations,
- Connections to prior or background knowledge,
- Focus on big ideas,
- Highlights of critical features (as in bold type or color-coded),
- Scaffolds and relationships,
- Time for information processing (can be individually paced),
- Reinforcement of memory (provides repetition),
- Prompts for recall (uses cues and reviews),
- Opportunities to generalize.

How does the student demonstrate knowledge?

Take into consideration the physical action, expressive and fluency skills, and executive functions necessary for students to show that they know. For example, the physical response typically required in writing an essay test may involve a unique means of navigation or responding such as using a switch and voice-activated software. The speed and accuracy with which the student can write would be involved in the expressive and fluency skills. Executive functions include those skills that support organizing thoughts and tasks required to accomplish the writing goal.

Assistive technology, including universally designed products and software, can be selected to support multiple:

- Methods of responding;
- Options to navigate;
- Media for communication;
- Tools for completing written responses;
- Models of problem solving, goal setting, planning, and strategizing;
- Opportunities to manage information and resources;
- Methods of assessment;
- Means of monitoring progress.

Special education teachers are trained to locate and design optional methods that ensure students are able to appropriately demonstrate knowledge.

How is the student motivated?

Appropriately applied assistive technology and universal design for learning can engage learners by challenging them while at the same time focusing on areas that are relevant and interesting to them. Factors that increase student motivation and support effort include the following:

- Providing choice
- Building authenticity
- Ensuring relevance
- Establishing goals
- Understanding and valuing the objective
- Using specific feedback that promotes mastery
- Varying the levels of challenge
- Designing opportunities for collaboration and communication
- Scaffolding reinforcement and coping strategies
- Encouraging self-assessment and personal reflection

Technology can be selected to align with the student's needs and still be learner-centered. Specific UDL guidelines can be found at: www.cast.org/publications/UDLguidelines.

Using Technology to Motivate Learners

Most students come to school with a history of computer use. The US Department of Education's National Center for Education Statistics (NCES) reported that 97 percent of kindergarteners had access to a computer at school or home (2003). Based on that same research, Internet use peaks between ages 12 and 15, and the fastest-growing population for Internet use is ages 2 to 5. Given these statistics, integration of technology into instructional practice is becoming a more natural method of engaging learners.

Teaching, Learning, and the Curriculum

The list of technological options is nearly unending, from software to new uses for common devices. Resources and contacts change rapidly, especially those available on the Internet. Update Web sites regularly. It is also important to ensure that Web sites provide accurate information, secure data collection, and meet high academic standards. Here are some common resources used by special education teachers:

Professional and Curriculum Resources

- http://www.cast.org/teachingeverystudent/—Templates, curriculum alignment options, and examples of effective use of UDL are found on the CAST Teaching Every Student Web site.

- www.mcrel.org or www.ncrel.org—Provides teachers with contemporary research, effective practices, and ideas for connecting content standards to instruction.
- www.cec.org—Identifies specific information related to disability areas, legal requirements, and political advocacy.
- www.do2Learn.org—The site is specifically related to instructional needs special education students have including support for content areas, language development, behavioral, and social concerns.

Interactive Options

- Electronic whiteboards provide interactive teaching and learning experiences. To learn more check http://www.eduscapes.com/sessions/smartboard/.
- www.thinkfinity.org—Offers free teaching resources for all content areas and activities are aligned with state content standards. Many of the activities are compatible with the SMARTboard and are interactive.

Text-to-Voice Options

- www.readplease.com—Free downloadable text-to-speech software.

Language Translation

- http://babelfish.yahoo.com—A convenient and free service to provide simple translations of many languages.

Student Engagement

- www.surveymonkey.com—Engage learners in creating simple opinion surveys or content inquiries.
- www.webquest.org—This Web site provides ideas for designing or embedding already developed Web quests. Web quests are similar to problems-based learning, where the teacher designs a situation related to the content. Students must navigate their way through Web sites to find an answer using hints or feedback provided by the teacher.
- www.efieldtrips.org—Free online field trips to museums and national or international spots.

Web Ideas

Web 2.0 is language for a two-way online experience. MySpace and Facebook, Wikis, and blogs are examples of a social experience. Their user-generated and user-created content sites are seen as proactive instructional approaches that are gaining popularity in the classroom. Among the strengths of Web 2.0 technologies are opportunities for student collaboration, student engagement, meaningful involvement, and ease of access.

- Wikis—An interactive space that can be reserved for a limited audience. Information shared is specific to a particular classroom and members must be invited into the site. Student work can be published and comments provided in a safe venue. For more information or to set up a Wiki go to: http://pbwiki.com/academic.wiki or http://www.wikispaces.com.
- Blogs—A blog can serve as a running record or history of events in a child's life or the life of a class. Some blogs are journals of educational events, and others serve as a soapbox for opinions. A blog has an international audience. Motivation to write and relevance to life are two strengths associated with blogging. Simultaneously, this requires ongoing teacher oversight and assurance that names and personal information are not divulged.
- www.YouTube.com offers a huge variety of video demonstrations describing how to incorporate technology in the classroom. Before incorporating YouTube, check to see if the school allows access. It is important to preview any video or Internet site before using it in class. "YouTube in Plain English," "Wikis in Plain English," and "Blogs in Plain English" are precise visual models of the power of technology.
- www.Skype.com is a video calling system to provide interactive conversations from one location to another via computer.

Podcasting

Academic options are increased by using podcasting. Podcasting is usually audio, but it can also be video. Students can be directed to listen to lectures, famous speeches, or descriptions of artwork on a podcast from a public radio Web site or other source by downloading the broadcast. Teachers can create a list of focused options on a content topic.

Student Response Systems (SRS) or Personal Response Systems (PRS)

These are also called "Clickers" and have become more prevalent in schools. The Clicker, approximately the size of a television remote, allows teachers and students to interact electronically during a class session. Questions are posed by the teacher to collect information on student comprehension.

Cell Phones

Texting is one process some educators are using to engage students in providing immediate feedback.

- http://twitter.com—Students can create a social group using four words, "What are you doing?" Twitter allows only "Tweaks," or short responses with less than 140 characters. One advantage to using Twitter is that social communities can be established for students with disabilities. The same question ("What are you doing?") is always asked, the network can be accessed by cell phone or Web, response lengths are limited, and the group of responders consists of individuals who know each other.

Electronic Whiteboards

Everything from math concepts to sign language can be enhanced using demonstrations on interactive whiteboards. Accommodations are easily made and incorporate many learning styles.

Digital Storytelling and Videocasting

Making movies to tell a story or sequence steps in learning a skill can be very motivating. Secondary special education teachers have sometimes provided visual and auditory details in transition plans using videos. Assessing progress can also be accomplished by providing a video of current performance.

Software

- Inspiration software provides graphic organizers useful for all content areas.
- Dragon NaturallySpeaking is software that is speech to text. It is fast and reliably records spoken language.
- Kurzweil is one example of software that has effectively incorporated the concept of UDL. Kurzweil software is designed to provide access to any curriculum at any grade level. It provides visual and auditory feedback, decoding support during reading, and provides tools for writing, editing and studying. Differentiated instruction is immediately available to students with disabilities, ELL students, or other struggling students.

Practice Prior to Purchasing

Prior to purchasing software or equipment for use with students it is important to try it out. Ask a representative of the company to demonstrate the product, which provides opportunity to learn detailed information from an expert. Take advantage of trial periods that allow you use the software for thirty days or longer. Evaluate the software, keeping in mind the student for whom it is intended. Consider the following questions:

- How do price and license requirements compare with a Web-based approach or other software?
- Is data protected? What security is included or needed?
- How is data collected and reported?
- What are hardware requirements?

Federal funds have been used to create parent organizations designed to educate and provide technical services for using technology. Specialists in the use of assistive technology are often available from these organizations to demonstrate devices. Technology, software, equipment, and tools may be available to try out before being purchased. One such organization is the Parent Advocacy Coalition for Educational Rights (PACER), located in Minnesota. They have a technology center that can be accessed at http://www.pacer.org/index.asp.

Depending on the academic and physical needs of students on your caseload, technology requirements could include head or mouth switches, orientation and mobility tools, or adapted physical education equipment. In order to successfully incorporate technology and use it effectively, training will be necessary.

SUMMARY

Technology is a constantly evolving option in education. Effective use of technology can increase professional productivity and enhance student learning. Legislation identifies assistive technology and universal design for learning as avenues to access and success. Teacher creativity in using technology promotes a variety of engaging student experiences to support achievement and maintain security. Rather than becoming overwhelmed by technology, identify and prioritize technology tools and practices that work for you and your students.

SELF-ASSESSMENT AND REFLECTION

After reading Chapter 7, please reflect on your knowledge and skill.

Self-Assessment

Respond to the following by answering Yes, Somewhat, or No.

I am able to:

_____ 1. Identify legal and practical reasons to incorporate technology,

_____ 2. Define and give examples of assistive technology (AT),

_____ 3. Integrate assistive technology to support students,

_____ 4. Explain universal design for learning (UDL),

_____ 5. Incorporate universal design for learning in instructional practice,

_____ 6. Identify technology that is used to motivate learners.

Reflection

1. Which of the self-assessment items do you feel fully competent in?

2. Which of the self-assessment items do you feel need some more work, emphasis, or study time?

3. Identify two specific actions that you can do to enrich and strengthen your instructional effectiveness.

eight—ocho—yim

Student Assessment and Evaluation

OBJECTIVES

1. Explain the difference between assessment and evaluation and provide two special education examples of each.

2. Explain the difference between formal and informal assessment and provide two special education examples of each.

3. Create effective rubrics.

4. Describe guidelines for preparing and implementing effective assessments.

5. Describe various levels of question prompts.

6. Describe several test-taking tips and strategies for students.

7. Distinguish between testing accommodations and modifications.

F ew aspects of instructional practice equal the importance of timely and accurate assessment and evaluation of student proficiency and progress. Years ago, many teachers tested students on what was taught. Today's protocol directs teachers to test students on information and skills that students are expected to achieve. That information and those skills are commonly described in national, state, and local principles such as standards, benchmarks, and performance indicators. With clear, concise, attainable, and measurable learning objectives, teachers are now better able to direct their instruction, including assessment and evaluation, toward helping their students attain the desired learning outcomes.

Given the focus and goals of *Powerful Practices for High-Performing Special Educators,* this chapter will focus on assessing and evaluating progress, achievement, and learning of students already in special education rather than on the initial identification and diagnosis of disabilities.

WISDOM OF PRACTICE: MS. THOMSON—WHAT'S IN A NUMBER?

Ms. Thomson gave a 20-question test to her eighth-grade science students. Zachary, one of her students, received a score of 16. Isabelle, another student, received a score of 12. Do the raw scores 16 and 12 represent an assessment or an evaluation?

Does the answer—assessment or evaluation—depend on whether the test was a pretest, midlesson test, or posttest? Does the answer vary depending on the learning diversity between Zachary and Isabelle?

The raw scores of 16 and 12 represent the mere gathering of data or information. Are the scores of 16 and 12 good scores or poor scores? That question is answered during the evaluation, or judgment, process. Is it possible that Isabelle's score of 12 represents more academic growth and progress than Zachary's score of 16? Absolutely. Isabelle's score may represent significant academic progress, whereas Zachary's score may represent little or no academic progress. The opposite scenario for Zachary and Isabelle could be true also. The professional interpretation and judgment by the teacher or other education professional is what determines the degree of learning significance.

Consider this analogy. Suppose an individual receives a medical check-up. Medical staffs commonly perform many tests such as blood pressure, blood chemistry, height, and weight. Many of these tests have numbers associated with them (such as 120/80). The gathering of these numbers represents an assessment. The meaning, interpretation, and judgment of the numbers by the professional medical staff represent the evaluation.

Do all medical assessments represent the same degree of significance or importance? Of course not. Some medical assessments may be of much more concern than others. Likewise, some educational assessments may represent a higher concern than others. In other words, not all assessments should, or do, represent an equal degree of educational significance.

In this chapter, the term *assessment* means the gathering of information related to the student's educational and learning proficiency and/or progress. The term *evaluation* means the professional interpretation and judgment of assessment information related to the student's educational and learning proficiency and/or progress. Evaluation follows assessment.

IN BRIEF: WHAT DOES THE RESEARCH SAY?

To ensure that students with disabilities are benefiting from education it is necessary to monitor progress. On-going assessments can be used to confirm achievement, change instruction, consider accommodations in order to access and benefit from the curriculum or, if necessary, change placement. The IEP should identify whether or not testing accommodations are needed, and, if so, the document should specify if the type, amount of time, or location of the classroom test changes. All students benefit from well-written and well-designed assessments. The link between instruction and assessment must be explicit. Instructional assessment confirms the match between effective teaching (what is taught and how it is taught) and student understanding. Grading is a concern that often comes up when students with disabilities are involved in classroom tests. A variety of grading options are available, including improvement scores and progress toward IEP goals (Friend & Bursuck, 2009). The increased level of accountability has multiplied the need to better prepare all teachers and students for high-stakes assessment (Thurlow, Elliot, & Yselldyke, 2003). Response to Intervention (RTI) is more often being used in districts to ensure that research-based instruction and assessment are employed as methods to reduce the number of students who might otherwise be referred to special education. Fairness is another concern sometimes expressed in conjunction with student assessment. For example, is it fair for students on IEPs to get named to the "A" Honor Roll? Students on IEPs should not be given a courtesy pass or a grade not earned; neither should they be discriminated against because of their disability. As a special education teacher it is important to provide opportunity to learn and equitable assessment to reinforce academic achievement for students on IEPs.

PROFESSIONAL PRACTICE

Among other things, IEPs designate the types of assessments, whether accommodations are needed, and how often progress is monitored and reported. Implementing a variety of assessments will help ensure appropriate instruction and achievement of goals.

Formal and Informal Assessment

Assessments can be either formal or informal. Formal assessments have specific data supporting the corresponding evaluation. Examples would include written tests and other academic performances. In general classroom terms, formal assessments typically contribute to the student's course evaluation or grade. Informal classroom assessments typically do not contribute directly to the student's course evaluation or grade. Common examples of informal assessments include teacher observations, discussions, self-assessment quizzes and inventories, and classroom participation.

Elements of Effective Assessment

For teachers, one of the more important factors needed for the creation of successful assessments is to be knowledgeable about, and apply, the elements that comprise effective assessments. Effective assessments have several distinct elements that can be identified and described. Teachers can use these elements as a checklist as they create or select and implement student assessments.

- ☐ *Authentic*—Assessments are related to real-life situations, circumstances, and tasks.

- ☐ *Varied*—Assessments are multidimensional and comprehensive. These include objective and subjective assessments, formal and informal assessments, formative and summative assessments, criterion-referenced and norm-referenced, and performance and demonstration assessments.

- ☐ *Valid*—Assessments measure the knowledge and skills they are intended to measure.

- ☐ *Reliable*—Assessments are dependable and consistent when administered to the same students on different occasions.

- ☐ *Feedback*—Assessments provide useful and timely responses and advice to students.

- ☐ *Developmental*—Assessments are appropriate to the intellectual, physical, and psychological maturity of the students.

- ☐ *Collaborative*—Assessments often involve the students as active participants in self- and peer assessing.

- ☐ *Focused*—Assessments match and measure the instructional objectives.

- ☐ *Planned*—Assessments are deliberate, purposeful, and intentional.

- ☐ *Systematic*—Assessments are well organized, efficient, and methodical.

- ☐ *Continuous or Ongoing*—Assessments occur on a daily and weekly basis throughout the lesson.

- ☐ *Seamless*—Assessments interact with, and are an integral part of, the curriculum and instruction; students are learning during the assessments.

- ☐ *Meaningful*—Assessments provide the student with the opportunity to produce information, products, or services.

- ☐ *Unbiased*—Assessments are equitable and fair, regardless of learning diversity.

- ☐ *Flexible*—Assessments focus on process as well as product.

- ☐ *Cumulative*—A longitudinal approach to assessment puts the results of any one assessment into perspective. A sampling of student work (portfolio) over time is one example of implementing a cumulative approach to assessment.

- ☐ *Diverse*—Assessments merge a variety of question types for the purpose of providing a more comprehensive representation of student achievement.

❏ *Performance Based*—Assessments involve student performances or demonstrations replicating what real people do in the real world.

❏ *Future Use*—Assessments can be directly applied to upcoming curriculum and instruction practices.

What to Assess?

With increasing learning diversity in today's classrooms teachers are often faced with the question, "What should I assess in my students?" Because of these diverse learning needs, many teachers are expected to assess students in areas reaching far beyond the specific content of the curriculum. Each of these objectives can be assessed. However, due to the diversity of the objectives, each objective should employ multiple and varied assessment techniques.

• *Content Objectives* define the essential knowledge (declarative/ procedural) of the discipline. These are typically characterized by facts, concepts, and/or skills. They clearly state what the learner is expected to know and/or be able to do.

• *Language Objectives* define the necessary communication skills (language modalities) needed to make the content of the discipline comprehensible. They identify what students should know and be able to do while using English. These are typically characterized by reading, writing, listening, and/or speaking.

• *Learning Strategies Objectives* define thinking and learning skills such as problem solving, analysis, synthesis, creativity, evaluation, attention and concentration, memory, motivation, note taking, proof reading, questioning, time management, test-taking strategies, and organization. Since these learning strategies can be taught and learned, they can be assessed.

• *Basic Skills Objectives* define the targeted skills, such as reading comprehension strategies and written and oral communication skills.

• *Social Affective Objectives* define the context in which learning can be achieved. These may include working with teachers and peers, preparing a time schedule, asking clarifying questions, cooperation, self-talk, self-monitoring, and locating and choosing conducive learning locations in the classroom—such as selecting a clear line for sight and hearing as well as selecting a location that reduces potential learning distractions.

Alternative, Authentic, and Performance Assessment

The terms alternative assessment, authentic assessment, and performance assessment are often used synonymously. However, they do have different meanings. Reviewing these terms will provide a more complete picture of assessment.

● *Alternative assessment* typically applies to all assessments different from the traditional, multiple-choice, true-false, matching, and completion type assessments. Alternative assessments encourage students to generate and construct their responses rather than select a right answer. In addition, alternative assessments allow the students to provide more complex information with the possibility for multiple explanations.

● *Authentic assessment* refers to assessments that ask students to apply their knowledge and skills to real-life, real-world situations, circumstances, and problems. Authentic assessments help students to see and better understand how their learning fits into what real people do in the real world. Self-assessments are often associated with authentic assessments.

● *Performance assessment* implies that students are asked to do some sort of activity such as demonstrating a skill, solving a multidimensional problem, or doing an arts performance. The basis of a performance assessment is to find out what the students can do and how well they can do it.

Diagnostic, Formative, and Summative Assessment

In simple terms, diagnostic assessments are designed to tell us what the student needs to learn. Formative assessments tell us how well the student is doing as his or her work progresses. Summative assessments tell us how well the student did at the end of a unit, major task, or term.

● *Diagnostic assessments* typically occur before instruction. Examples include pretests, observations, journals/logs, discussions, placement tests, standardized tests, questionnaires, checklists, behavior inventories, video, or audiotapes. In special education, diagnostic tests can include those designed for very specific academic needs including communication skills, writing, reading, math, social skills, emotional health, physical capabilities, or functional activities. For every area there are corresponding standardized curriculum assessments (see, for instance, KeyMath, Brigance) designed to be used as components in making decisions for instruction. Diagnostic assessments help identify consistent errors, misunderstandings, or gaps in knowledge that need to be taught.

● *Formative assessments* typically occur and are ongoing during instruction. Examples include quizzes, discussions, assignments, projects, teacher-made tests, checklists, probes, observations, portfolios, journals/logs, and standardized tests. Other methods special education teachers use to determine student progress are student-led conferences to discuss goals, self-assessments, and homework with immediate, constructive teacher feedback.

● *Summative assessments* typically occur at the end of instruction. Examples include teacher-made tests, portfolios, projects, standardized tests, interviews, discussions, and a wide variety of performances. Often, special educators use task analysis to create the steps of a procedure that must be mastered by a student on an IEP.

The criteria and conditions are written into the student's educational plan and most include generalization and maintenance. When the objectives are met, new goals are written. IEP goals are reviewed at least annually as part of a summative assessment to ensure accountability for academic progress during the year.

Developing Effective Rubrics

A rubric is an instrument for organizing and interpreting criteria-driven data gathered from student assignments, tasks, observations, and performances. Assessment rubrics are often provided to students along with their academic assignments or tasks. A rubric will clearly define the basis for how their assignment will be evaluated and graded. For students with disabilities, rubrics provide a detailed structure of expectations that are aligned with standards and reinforce IEP goals.

As teachers create rubrics, they may want to check to see if their State Department of Education offers model rubrics related to state and/or national standards.

Two common types of rubrics include *analytic* rubrics and *holistic* rubrics. Analytic rubrics identify the multiple and individual components of a finished assignment. Holistic rubrics assess the assignment as a whole. Is one type better than the other? Each type has advantages. Many students, especially special education students and English language learners, prefer analytic rubrics because the rubric details the specific requirements of the assignment. Many teachers use holistic rubrics with students who prefer to approach and complete the assignment from a more comprehensive view by considering all the different aspects of the assignment in a more global sense.

The analytic rubric will typically include several assignment components such as grammar accuracy, information accuracy, quality of information, quantity of information, sources of information, and creativity. Obviously, the type of assignment will dictate the rubric components. For example, the rubric's components for a speech or other physical performance would be different from the rubric's components for a research report or art project.

Each component of a rubric defines a specific level of student performance relative to that component. Commonly, four levels are used. Teachers use a variety of ways to define these levels. (See Tables 8.1 and 8.2, following.)

Table 8.1	Four-Level Rubric

Criteria Example	Distinguished	Proficient	Basic	Unacceptable
Organization				
Word Choice				
Ideas				
Sentence Fluency				

Table 8.2 Three-Level Rubric

Criteria Example	Meets Standard	Developing	Not Yet
Organization			
Word Choice			
Ideas			
Sentence Fluency			

Some teachers prefer a rubric with a range of four levels of student performance (Table 8.1), whereas others prefer a range of three levels of student performance (Table 8.2). When using either a four-level or three-level rubric, the teacher can select the most appropriate terms and combinations to describe and reflect the various levels of student performance the teacher is targeting. Each term should be clearly and precisely defined to the students.

There are several terms that can be used to identify the specific levels of student performance, such as

- outstanding, excellent, high, distinguished, meets standard;
- acceptable, good, above average, proficient;
- needs improvement, below average, basic;
- unacceptable, poor, low, unsatisfactory.

Some teachers simply use numbers (Table 8.3) such as 4, 3, 2, 1 or 3, 2, 1.

Table 8.3 Criteria and Number Rubric

Criteria Example	4	3	2	1
Organization				
Word Choice				
Ideas				
Sentence Fluency				

Some teachers choose to combine the performance level terms and numbers (Table 8.4) such as

- Excellent (4)
- Above Average (3)
- Below Average (2)
- Unacceptable (1)

Table 8.4 Criteria With Term and Number Rubric

Criteria Example	Excellent 4	Above Average 3	Below Average 2	Unacceptable 1
Organization				
Word Choice				
Ideas				
Sentence Fluency				

Teachers who choose to include numbers (4, 3, 2, 1 or 3, 2, 1) in each criterion often add up the total of numbers and then translate that total into a letter grade. See Table 8.5 for an example of a writing rubric.

Using Table 8.5 as an example of assessment number to grade, the teacher would add up the assessment points (4 + 3 + 3 + 4 + 2) to get 16 total points. The teacher would then create a grading scale based on a total 20 possible (4 points × 5 criteria) assessment points. An example would be:

18–20 = A

15–17 = B

12–14 = C

< 12 = Not Passing

Table 8.5 Sample Writing With Scoring Rubric

Criteria Example	Distinguished 4	Proficient 3	Basic 2	Unacceptable 1
Appropriate Vocabulary	X			
Writing Is Organized		X		
Purpose Is Clear		X		
Correct Mechanics	X			
Writing Is Neat			X	

There are several Web sites, such as http://rubistar.4teachers.org/index.php, that offer excellent prototypes and ideas to assist teachers in creating rubrics. Many of these Web sites offer rubric examples in a wide range of grade levels, ability levels, and academic disciplines.

Weighting Assignments and Projects

Teachers have long realized that the various components and grading criteria that comprise more robust student assignments are not of equal value in terms of assessing, evaluating, and grading. Weighting an assignment means applying a degree of importance or significance to the various components of a student assignment or project. For example, a teacher may use this list of grading criteria for a written report:

- Capitalization and Punctuation
- Spelling and Grammar
- Paragraph Transitions
- Accuracy of Information
- Amount of Information
- Sources of Information
- Diagrams and Illustrations

Depending on the specific student learning objectives, the teacher may choose to place a higher degree of emphasis on some of the criteria components and less emphasis on others. How can a teacher organize the student criteria information that reflects the emphasis the teacher desires?

Using the seven criteria items listed above as an example, the teacher first assigns a number—1, 2, or 3—to each criterion. The number 1 represents a low emphasis, 2 represents a medium emphasis, and 3 represents a high (most important) emphasis. See Step 1 example.

Step 1	
Emphasis	**Criteria Item**
3	Capitalization and Punctuation
3	Spelling and Grammar
1	Paragraph Transitions
2	Accuracy of Information
2	Amount of Information
1	Sources of Information
1	Diagrams and Illustrations

When students have the opportunity to see and understand this emphasis, it provides them with a focus on where to concentrate their effort as they complete their assignment. They know what the teacher is going to focus on when giving the assignment a grade.

The next step happens when the teacher assesses and evaluates the students' work. The teacher applies a single number (3, 2, 1, 0) that represents the degree to which the student achieved each criteria item. 3 = high achievement, 2 = moderate achievement, 1 = low achievement, 0 = no achievement. See Step 2 example.

Step 2		
Emphasis	Criteria Item	Achievement
3	Capitalization and Punctuation	3
3	Spelling and Grammar	2
1	Paragraph Transitions	0
2	Accuracy of Information	1
2	Amount of Information	3
1	Sources of Information	3
1	Diagrams and Illustrations	2

The final step involves multiplying the Emphasis Score × Achievement Score and then adding the total. See Step 3 example.

Step 3			
Emphasis	Criteria Item	Achievement	Score
3	Capitalization & Punctuation	3	9
3	Spelling and Grammar	2	6
1	Paragraph Transitions	0	0
2	Accuracy of Information	1	2
2	Amount of Information	3	6
1	Sources of Information	3	3
1	Diagrams and Illustrations	2	2
			Total=28

The student receives an assignment score of 28 (out of a possible 39). The teacher can then determine what the score of 28 means in terms of student achievement and a grade.

As you can see, this method allows the teacher to weight (apply importance or significance) each component of a student assignment. This will also allow the student to focus on the assignment's most important elements. A rubric is used to define and describe the achievement levels (3, 2, 1, 0) that correspond to each criterion.

Preparing and Implementing Effective Assessments

There are several reasons why teachers prepare student tests. Some of the more common reasons are:

- To establish a basis for assigning grades,
- To determine how well each student has achieved the learning objectives,
- To diagnose student learning problems or barriers,
- To determine where the teacher's instruction needs improvement,
- To determine the effectiveness of a specific curriculum or student assignment.

Regardless of the purpose, teacher-prepared tests should be effective in gathering the desired student information.

One way to prepare and implement effective student assessments is to have a predetermined strategy. Student assessments (gathering information) should focus on the student's learning objectives and expectations. Content assessments typically ask the students to reply to questions or ask the student to complete a project or demonstration.

The student's learning objectives will dictate the assessment type and strategy. Teachers will often select some type of objective assessment when testing students on the recall of information. With this type of assessment, students typically can select an answer from a list of possible answers such as in a multiple-choice type of question. There is only one correct answer. Objective tests can often be electronically scored, saving the teacher considerable "correcting" time. There are advantages, disadvantages, and preparation guidelines to the familiar types of objective tests. However, for some students, building testing confidence is a higher priority than the correct answer. Therefore, in these special circumstances, some of the testing guidelines may have to be customized or altered. (Preparing and Implementing Effective Assessments adapted, with permission, from M. Bergs' 2005 consulting service, *Working with English Language Learners, LLC)*

Choosing the type of test questions will depend on the learner objectives and instructional methods. Advantages and disadvantages can serve as guidelines when making a decision about the type of assessment questions to use.

TRUE—FALSE

Advantages: Can cover many items in a short time, easy to score.

Disadvantages: Tend to oversimplify ideas or mislead if not written carefully.

Guidelines:

- Include a large number of items, more than twice the number of multiple-choice, for instance. This compensates for the 50 percent guessing factor and takes advantage of the strength of this type of test.
- Include one idea per item and keep the statement short.
- Write your own sentences. Do not copy sentences directly from textbooks; they are out of context.
- Test important ideas, not trivia. Factual material, such as definition of terms, is better tested with multiple choice or matching to decrease the high guess factor.
- Avoid verbal clues. "Never," "always," and "every" tend to make statements false. "Often," "usually," and "frequently" tend to make true statements. True statements tend to be longer than false statements.
- A good technique is to have students revise false statements to make them correct. However, this makes scoring more difficult.

MATCHING

Advantages: Useful when the same options fit several multiple-choice stems.

Disadvantages: Tend to be limited to factual knowledge.

Guidelines:

- Every option should be a plausible answer to every stem. A well-constructed matching set could be replaced by several multiple-choice items with identical options.
- Put the stem on the left (numbered) and the options on the right (lettered).
- Avoid having the same number of items and options, with each option used only once. (Exception: When building testing confidence, it may be best to have an equal number.)
- If there is a logical sequence to the options, place them in order.

MULTIPLE CHOICE

Advantages: Can be used to measure many objectives—including higher-level reasoning—easy to score.

Disadvantages: Difficult to construct. Not capable of measuring creative, divergent thinking.

(Continued)

(Continued)

Guidelines:

- Ask the question in the stem. In most cases, the student should be able to answer the question without reading the options.
- Be sure that the options deal with alternatives to a single concept. Do not try to test several different concepts in one question.
- Eliminate unnecessary wordiness in both the stem and the options. Do not include long explanations. Do not use the test to teach some extra information. Be sure that the right answer is not longer than the wrong options.
- The stem may be a question or an incomplete statement. Questions are preferred as they are usually clearer. Do not invert the wording. Ask the question directly. If an incomplete statement, put the blank at the end of the sentence, not at the beginning or in the middle. After a question, options begin with capital letters; in an incomplete sentence, options begin with small letters.
- Be sure that each option is plausible. They must not overlap. There must be clearly one right answer. Do not include obviously ridiculous answers; save the reading time. You may vary the number of options to questions.
- Avoid negatively phrased stems. If you occasionally use a negative word, underline it. Never use a negative stem and negative options in the same item.
- Avoid "all of the above" or "none of the above." Two right answers are a clue to "all of the above." Recognizing wrong options does not prove knowledge of right options.
- Avoid verbal clues in the stem or in the options. Be sure the grammar is appropriate within each option.
- Arrange options in a logical order. Follow the thinking pattern, if there is an order evident. Use a vertical rather than a horizontal arrangement.
- Avoid writing "which of the following . . . "

COMPLETION

Advantages: Useful where a clear, short answer is required. Reduces the possibility of guessing.

Disadvantages: Tends to measure only recall information.

Guidelines:

- Do not take sentences directly from the textbook.
- The best items are a question followed by a blank for the response.
- Construct the question so that the answer is definite and brief.
- Do not write a sentence with several blanks.
- Avoid grammatical clues in incomplete sentences.
- If you put blanks in sentences, make them all the same length.

ESSAY

As opposed to the question types previously listed, essay questions often require students to make decisions, suggest strategies to solve problems, organize information, or defend positions.

Advantages: Can be used to assess the ability to organize thoughts and compose ideas. Assesses creative and divergent thinking.

Disadvantages: Difficult to write, hard to score reliability, provides limited coverage of content. Time-consuming scoring. Student scores may be influenced by their writing ability or lack thereof.

- Construct the question simply and clearly to direct the students to the desired response.
- Give the students as much information about the requirements of a correct response as you can.
- Make a checklist that can be used to grade all tests.
- Prepare an answer when you write the question. It will help you see any needed revision of the question.
- If you find yourself beginning the question with words such as "list," "who," "what," and "how many," a series of objective items would probably be more effective. Use essay questions when the students' thought processes are important in assessment.
- The amount of time to be spent on each question and the point value should be indicated. Then be sure to follow your rules.
- Avoid having students select which questions to answer.

In addition to selecting and preparing appropriate questions, teachers must also consider testing directions, time, sequence, chunking, and white space.

- Directions: Teachers should provide clear general directions for the test. Is a special pencil or marker required? Where should the student put his or her identifying information such as name, course, or period? Is there an answer sheet or do the students put their answers on the test? How will the various testing items be graded or scored? In addition, each set of questions within the test should have their own specific directions. Separating the directions from the questions using different color, font, style, or bold type is often helpful.
- Time: Teachers should provide students with a clear understanding of the time allowed for the test. Make sure students have enough time to complete the test.
- Sequence: How will the questions be sequenced? Many teachers prefer to place the easier questions at the beginning of the test and the more difficult questions at the end of the test. Each question in the entire test should be numbered consecutively.

- Chunking: How will the questions and required reading be broken up into manageable sections? For example, long sentences may cause the student to forget the sentence beginning by the time he gets to the end of the sentence. Chunked assessments (and other reading material) can improve comprehension of many readers—especially struggling readers.
- White Space: The visual appearance of the assessment can influence the student's success and confidence. Many struggling students have greater test-taking confidence when they see an assessment with significant white space—the empty space that surrounds the text. White space can create a more relaxing testing environment for the student. When preparing student assessments, teachers are therefore encouraged to also think about the assessment's visual appearance, not just the assessment's quantity.

And, finally, just because a question or test is located in the teacher's edition of the textbook does not mean that the question or test appropriately matches the student's learning objectives. Teachers should be carefully selective when preparing student questions.

QUESTION PROMPTS

Question prompts, as part of an assessment program, are helpful ways to focus students on specific information. Question prompts are sometimes called question starters. Question prompts are used to trigger student responses. The prompts can produce lower-level thinking as well as higher-level thinking responses. Listed below are sample question prompts adapted, with permission, from M. Bergs (2005) *Working with English Language Learners, L.L.C.* They range from prompts that require a lower level of cognitive response to prompts that require a higher level of cognitive response.

1. Who _____?
2. How did _____?
3. What is _____?
4. When did _____?
5. Where is _____?
6. Describe _____.
7. Retell _____ in your own words.
8. What is the main idea of _____?
9. How are _____ alike/different?
10. What can you say about _____?

11. What is the best answer _____?

12. Arrange _____ in order.

13. Give reasons for _____.

14. What if _____?

15. Find an example of _____.

16. How can you solve _____?

17. How can you use _____?

18. Show your understanding of _____ by _____.

19. How is _____ an example of _____?

20. How is _____ related to _____?

21. Why is _____ significant?

22. What are the parts or features of _____?

23. Classify _____ according to _____.

24. Outline _____.

25. Create a graphic organizer of _____.

26. Compare and contrast _____ and _____.

27. What evidence do you have for _____?

28. What does _____ say about _____?

29. What would you predict from _____?

30. How would you create a _____?

31. What ideas can you add to _____?

32. What would happen if you combined _____ with/and_____?

33. What solutions would you suggest for _____?

34. How can we improve _____?

35. What is another way to _____?

36. What would happen if _____?

37. Do you agree with _____?

38. What do you think about _____?

39. Would it be better to _____ or _____?

40. What is the most important part of _____?

41. How would you decide about _____?

Test-Taking Tips and Strategies

Ideally, all teachers want their students to learn and be successful. Test-taking tips and strategies are generic ways to assist students in their assessment process and can increase their likelihood of success. Test-taking tips do NOT include giving answers to students during the test, but rather providing a helpful and supportive pretest process.

Teachers, parents, and students all have specific responsibilities and obligations to ensure the greatest testing success.

Teachers

Teachers can provide several test-taking strategies designed to help students. These include:

- Informing students of important testing dates well in advance,
- Establishing a favorable classroom-testing environment,
- Establishing and explaining specific test-behavior guidelines,
- Establishing and explaining specific testing time limits,
- Explaining all unfamiliar requirements and directions,
- Explaining the orderly test collection process.

Parents

During parent-teacher conferences and other communications with parents, teachers can offer testing support strategies for parents to use when helping their children prepare for important tests. These include:

- Marking important test dates on the home calendar,
- Encouraging their child to study and complete homework,
- Scheduling medical and other appointments on nontest days,
- Providing a quiet study area,
- Providing a good night's rest prior to the testing day,
- Providing a good breakfast on the testing day,
- Making sure their child arrives at school on time,
- Making sure their child has all the required testing materials (pencils, notebooks, and so on).
- Asking their child about the test when he or she returns home.

Students

Students have a major responsibility when preparing for an important test. There are several test-taking strategies that can be, and should be, utilized. Teachers should share these strategies with their students. These include:

- Keeping up with good study habits and completing homework,
- Keeping class information and assignments organized,
- Getting a good night's sleep and eating a healthy breakfast before the test,
- Bringing all necessary testing materials to class,
- Reading and following the testing directions,
- Knowing if there is a penalty for guessing,

- Reading each question carefully,
- Reading every possible answer,
- Not spending too much time on any one question,
- Writing legibly,
- Checking over their answers if time permits,
- Asking the teacher for additional test-taking strategies,
- Thinking positively and confidently.

Grading Students on IEPs

Assigning grades to students on IEPs is an important discussion. Grading systems are used as indicators of achievement, progress, effort, motivation, and eligibility for such things as extracurricular activities or graduation. Issues related to grading may have legal implications. For instance, the designation "modified grade" or "Resource Room Math" are not permitted as part of a transcript (Salend & Duhaney, 2002). Many of the assessment practices described in this chapter coordinate nicely with the contemporary use of standards and differentiation in assessment. Additional considerations when it comes to grading include:

- Regularly informing families of the student's progress (done as often as peers receive report cards or as designated on the IEP),
- Involving students in the grading process by using self-evaluation,
- Reviewing grading policies and practices with staff.

Revised grading procedures may constitute an accommodation that would be specified on a student's IEP.

Distinguish Between Testing Accommodations and Modifications

The intensity of the student's disability and his or her educational needs serve as a starting point when planning instruction. Ongoing assessment ensures progress can be documented. Federal legislation requires that the majority of students with disabilities be included in accountability assessments. The IEP process provides the mechanism for teams to collaboratively assess and identify accommodations necessary to mitigate the effects of the disability. IEPs are written to ensure that students have access to general education curriculum and their progress is documented.

A growing area of interest for school districts is that of "allowable" accommodations for the purposes of testing. It is important to know the difference between testing accommodations and modifications. Accommodations and modifications are actually two very different concepts, even though people sometimes use them interchangeably.

An accommodation is a change in the way a test is administered without altering the content of the test. Accommodations are intended to maximize a student's performance and to "obtain an accurate picture of the student's true capabilities" (Horvath, Kampfer-Bohach, & Kearns, 2005, p. 178). Accommodations are typically made in four categories, which are as follows:

1. Time
   o More time in one setting
   o More frequent breaks
   o Allowing the test to be taken over several days

2. Setting
   o In a special education classroom or other location (library, home, or hospital with accountability factors in place)
   o Special lighting
   o Sitting at a study carrel
   o Working in a small group
   o Using a headset to reduce noise distractions

3. Presentation Format
   o Braille
   o Large print
   o More white space
   o Test directions—signed, interpreted, or audio-taped
   o Highlighted key words

4. Response Format
   o Using a computer
   o Writing in the test booklet
   o Responding in sign language
   o Pointing to a response
   o Using pictures or other fixed template ("Yes"/"No" for true and false responses; or "A, B, C, D" for multiple choice questions)

An accommodation holds the student with a disability to the same goals and standards established for the general population. Test modifications, however, change essential elements, or constructs, of the test (Bolt & Thurlow, 2004). A test modification might include omitting whole sections or substituting items on a test. Test modifications are often applied equally across a variety of students without any consideration of a learner's individual needs (such as answer only the odd-numbered questions; complete the True and False section only; eliminate the essay portion of the assessment). If a learner has significant disabilities such that a test is modified substantially, IEP teams must consider if the student needs to participate in the state's alternate assessment. In addition, if the child has a home language other than English, the team must consider administering assessments in the native language.

Each state is to have a policy on assessment accommodations. Researchers have noted that state guidelines have limited consensus, may be inconsistently applied, are sometimes ambiguous, and are constantly evolving (Horvath et al., 2005; Thompson & Thurlow, 2001). Some state guidelines identify an extensive list of accommodations. Other state policies simply note "extended time" without identifying any parameters, or permit "assistive technology" without giving examples. Most states include disclaimers suggesting the list is not exclusive and would allow other assessment accommodations if they did not give an unfair advantage to the student with a disability (Horvath et al., 2005).

Teacher knowledge of what is being tested and the allowable accommodations is critical. The seven most frequently allowed accommodations in state guidelines are as follows:

1. Individual administration

2. Small group administration of a test

   (Both 1 and 2 are allowed as routine test standardization procedures.)

3. Dictated response (to a scribe)

4. Large print

5. Braille

6. Extended time (considered by many teachers to maintain the test integrity)

7. Using an interpreter (signing) for instructions (Bolt & Thurlow, 2004)

The commonality across states does not necessarily coincide with frequency of use, effectiveness of use, or necessity for the accommodation.

Keep in mind two key factors when making decisions about testing accommodations:

1. An accommodation is allowed if it is documented on the student's IEP. An accommodation should be individualized.

2. An accommodation is permitted for use during assessment if the student also uses it during classroom instruction. Be consistent in applying the accommodation from the IEP to instruction and assessment.

Students, to the extent possible, should be involved in the accommodation decision. When students are proactive rather than passive, selection and use of accommodations in demonstrating learning becomes more authentic. Accommodations made available at a variety of levels support the concept of self-determination researched by Wehmeyer, Agran, & Hughes (2000). Self-determination skills include choice making, self-regulation, self-management, decision making, goal setting, self-monitoring, self-reinforcement, and self-direction. These skills must be specifically taught. Once learned, self-determination impacts all academic, social, and functional areas, including assessment of progress similar to peers.

SUMMARY

Effective and efficient teaching is based on identifying specific and measurable learning objectives, teaching to those objectives, and assessing students to determine the degree of their achievement of the objectives. With conscientious and appropriate assessment, teachers will be able to determine whether or not the scope and sequence of their instruction can move forward. Sometimes a review or reteaching lesson is needed.

SELF-ASSESSMENT AND REFLECTION

After reading Chapter 8, please reflect on your knowledge and skill.

Self-Assessment Items

Respond to the following by answering Yes, Somewhat, or No.

I am able to:

_____ 1. Explain the difference between assessment and evaluation and provide two special education examples of each,

_____ 2. Explain the difference between formal and informal assessment and provide two special education examples of each,

_____ 3. Create effective rubrics,

_____ 4. Describe guidelines for preparing and implementing effective assessments,

_____ 5. Describe various levels of question prompts,

_____ 6. Describe several test-taking tips and strategies for students,

_____ 7. Distinguish between testing accommodations and modifications.

Reflection

1. Which of the self-assessment items do you feel fully competent in?

2. Which of the self-assessment items do you believe need some more work, emphasis, or study time?

3. Identify two specific actions you can take to enrich and strengthen your instructional effectiveness.

9

nine—nueve—cuaj

Promoting Achievement Through Collaboration

OBJECTIVES

1. Identify attributes of successful collaborators.

2. Describe roles and responsibilities in collaborative teams.

3. Identify and use collaborative practices when working with general education teachers, families, and others.

4. Use practices that enhance collaboration.

Special educators recognize both the value and challenges of collaboration. In educational settings, opportunities are presented daily to work together. Much has been written about the value of collaboration when working with students on Individualized Education Programs (IEPs). General and special education teachers benefit from the support they each receive as they work together to plan for and teach all students. Parents who are engaged as partners throughout assessment and program development understand and support the outcome.

Despite the benefits, professionals note they often experience resistance on many different levels and from a variety of sources. Collaboration may require challenging misconceptions. Recognizing barriers prepares special educators to be proactive in addressing the needs of students. Building relationships and effectively communicating information are two practices necessary for collaboration. Successful collaborators reflect on their practices and skills.

Collaboration takes many forms as roles and responsibilities are determined in the context of a student's educational goals. Collaborative learning communities consisting of special education and general education teachers, English language learner (ELL) teachers, administrators, related services, and paraprofessionals can be designed to identify and reinforce student achievement.

WISDOM OF PRACTICE: MRS. STANTON'S BEST-LAID PLANS

Sylvia Gomez's mother was scheduled to come for an IEP meeting after school. Mrs. Stanton, the new special education teacher, had sent written notice of the meeting ten days in advance (and e-mail reminders) to the principal, the ELL teacher, the school psychologist, the social worker, Sylvia's fourth-grade teacher, Mrs. Rivera, and next year's fifth-grade teacher, Mr. Newsome. Mr. Newsome rarely came to IEP meetings and often made comments to Mrs. Stanton such as, "It doesn't matter what I think. Do what you want, just tell me what to do."

Fifteen minutes before the meeting was to begin, Mrs. Stanton's phone rang. It was Mr. Newsome. He apologized but said he was unable to attend Sylvia's meeting. Mrs. Stanton managed an "Okay." When Mrs. Rivera walked into the room a few minutes later, Mrs. Stanton mentioned how defeated she felt by Mr. Newsome's behavior. When Mrs. Rivera asked what collaborative attempts had been initiated with Mr. Newsome, Mrs. Stanton drew a blank. After the meeting, Mrs. Rivera and Mrs. Stanton brainstormed ideas to assist in building a collaborative relationship with Mr. Newsome.

Many new special educators need guidance in developing practices supportive of collaboration. Successful collaborators devote time and energy in order to create environments where responsibilities are meaningfully implemented to increase the opportunity for student achievement.

IN BRIEF: WHAT DOES THE RESEARCH SAY?

The emphasis on collaboration is a result of the ongoing need for normalization of students with disabilities. Solutions to difficult situations can often be found through the unique perspectives of the various experts involved. It is expected that more collaborative practices and higher-quality teaching will result in improved student achievement. Collaboration has been researched and written about extensively. Marilyn Friend and Lynne Cook (2007) note that collaboration is a voluntary engagement between at least two individuals. Collaboration involves effective communication, goal setting, decision making, and problem solving. Collaborative efforts are meaningful only when they help educators function in ways that promote student learning (Brownell, Adams, Sindelar, Waldron, & Vanhover, 2006). According to DuFour (2004) the real test of collaboration is when teachers focus on knowing how each student learns rather than asking what they are expected to teach students.

Defining Collaboration

The term "collaboration" has often been used interchangeably with such other nouns as partnership or team. Collaboration, in some situations, has been used as a synonym for verbs such as communicate or interact. Mistakenly, some educators equate collaboration with coteaching, consulting, cooperation, or coordination.

For the purposes of this chapter, we will use a definition of collaboration that addresses diverse students with special education needs. *Collaboration is the active engagement of two or more professionals who bring their knowledge and experience together, and, in tandem with family input, systematically plan, design, instruct, assess, and evaluate student educational goals.* From this definition it is important to note the various components:

1. Collaboration is knowledge and skill.

2. There is engagement that requires discussion and action.

3. Collaboration is a continuous process.

4. The student's educational success is the foundation of the collaboration.

Each person comes into the collaborative moment with a history of professional and personal experiences, diverse understandings, academic strengths, available resources, materials, and expectations for students. It is important to consider these as assets that can strengthen the instruction designed for students.

Collaboration: Legislative Foundations

Special educators recognize and support the idea of being a member of an educational team. Teaming was identified repeatedly in Public Law 94:142 when students with disabilities were afforded by law a free, appropriate, public education. The language of the law includes parent participation, the use of a multidisciplinary team for assessment and diagnosis, and decisions made on information from more than one setting, from more than one person, and from more than one assessment. Legislation specifies that parents, general and special educators, an administrator, an individual who can discuss the implications of the assessments, and, where appropriate, students should be present at Individual Education Program (IEP) meetings. Historically, collaboration has been established and supported through congressional acts and legal precedence.

PROFESSIONAL PRACTICE

Most new special education teachers do not anticipate needing much, if any, support with collaboration. Sometimes successful collaboration is associated with personality traits or characteristics such as being easy to get along with, being a good listener, being goal oriented, asking questions, and sharing information. Positive personal characteristics are helpful for effective collaboration, but there is more to it. Collaboration is a dynamic process that requires ongoing personal reflection.

Attributes of Successful Collaborators

There are a number of characteristics aligned with successful collaborators. How do you rate yourself on the characteristics in Table 9.1?

Table 9.1 Self-Assessment: Successful Collaborators

I am:	Low 1	Medium 2	High 3
1. enthusiastic about entering into collaborative teaching;			
2. student-centered and focused on student learning;			
3. caring and have a holistic view of students;			
4. knowledgeable, skilled, and have expertise in my licensure area;			
5. secure, excited, and confident in a collaborating role;			
6. flexible, open, willing to share teaching strategies and learning activities, and to compromise and change;			
7. able to offer a high level of professionalism and respect to the collaborating partner and students;			
8. committed to shared responsibility and accountability;			
9. excited about the potential of a more flexible and creative use of time;			
10. able to listen and ask questions;			
11. excited about knowing more about *all* the students;			
12. excited about a greater shared ownership of students and student learning;			

I am:	Low 1	Medium 2	High 3
13. excited about an increased reflection on instructional practice;			
14. excited about increased collective expertise;			
15. looking forward to decreasing teacher isolation;			
16. excited about increased instructional support;			
17. excited about the possibility of having more energy and a greater enjoyment of teaching;			
18. looking forward to setting teaching goals.			
Total Score =			

When finished, add up the numbers in each column, and then total the score. Based on this self-assessment, the higher a number, the more attributes you have for being a successful collaborator. If your score was lower than you anticipated, it may be important to review your collaboration characteristics. Look at the items where you scored one or two. Are there places where you can change some behaviors and boost your score?

Individual qualities and characteristics are a launching point for growing great teams. Strong student assessments and instructional opportunities are the product of honest reflection as an individual as well as in group discussion. Decisions are made as a result of the interplay between personal and team responses to collaborative concepts of knowledge, disclosure, and acceptance.

Overcoming Perceptions

Collaboration is sometimes clouded by perceptions of others. An attitude may be shaped by a previous experience, an observation, or gossip. Some perceptions are related to differences in professional status, skill and ability, personality traits, style of work, communication skills, and diversity. Successful collaborators are able to overcome perceptions and negative thoughts. They often

- Focus on strengths collaborative partners bring to the situation.
- Use positive self-talk.
- Create an action plan to change negative thinking.

- Look for opportunities to be successful and celebrate.
- Where there are differences or conflicts, find ways to use them as a process for growing and learning.

In a collaborative situation, working with someone similar in background, philosophy, or instructional style may be most desirable, but it is not always feasible. Collaboration often occurs with two people unlike each other. Individual weaknesses are reduced as collaborative teams become stronger. Personal strengths surface and enhance team qualities. The goal of collaboration is to develop a network to support student achievement. Teams are woven together through ongoing discussion, disagreements, and compromise. It is a process that involves communication, feedback, and trust.

Collaboration is stronger as a result of the relationships that are developed with diverse individuals. Teachers who open the doors of their classrooms have the opportunity to grow through collaborative experiences. Collaboration is an opportunity to see things from another's perspective.

The Special Educator's Role and Responsibility in Collaborative Teams

Consider the following typical collaborative teams. Each has a specific function in the life of a special education teacher and a student with disabilities. Throughout the course of a week, a special educator shifts between many teams and roles.

- *A Teacher Assistance Team (TAT)*—This type of team identifies instructional strategies and behavioral supports that might be keys to a student's needs in the general classroom. Sometimes these teams go by other names such as Student Assistance Team (SAT) or Student Support Team (SST). The TAT designs a prereferral intervention and data collection focused on a clearly identified concern. A special education teacher may serve as a consultant in suggesting effective academic or behavioral interventions.

- *A Child Study Team (CST)* —Child study meetings are intended to provide a multidisciplinary perspective. Special educators, related services professionals, administrators, and general teachers meet regularly to consider the status of student referrals. Decisions are made to follow up with initial assessments and schedule reevaluations as required by law. Special education teachers plan and facilitate the discussion of students who are referred for special education. Your role is to invite team members and keep a record of the meeting and comments made by teachers, counselors, nurses, school psychologists, social workers, and speech, occupational, and physical therapists.

- *An IEP Team*—The special education teacher coordinates all aspects of the assessment and due process procedures associated with the identification of a disability and educational decisions made by the IEP team. Parent(s) or guardian(s), regular and special education teachers, related services professionals, an administrator, community members, ELL interpreters, and, if appropriate, the young person with the disability, may be involved in an IEP meeting as you design education to benefit the child. A key collaborative component is to keep members engaged in discussion around the needs of the child rather than simply looking for a label and a placement.

- *Department or Grade-Level Team*—In some settings, special educators are aligned with math, English, science, other content areas, or a grade-level, rather than remaining a separate department. As a special educator assigned to one of these teams, you will participate as an equal partner in discussions about course scheduling, standards linked to curriculum, and instructional practice and their impact on students with disabilities. Your expertise includes knowledge of disabilities, accommodations, assistive technology, and other special education topics others will find valuable.

- *A Coteaching Team*—Collaboration might mean you are involved in coteaching. Your roles and responsibilities will need to be determined. Discuss how you will be actively engaged in designing effective instruction, teaching, assessment, and communicating the needs and progress of students. Determine if your role is to provide consultation to the teacher, direct support to a student, or something in between. Part of your role is to assist the coteacher in developing a stronger relationship with and responsibility for students on IEPs who are in general education classrooms.

- *ELL/Special Education Team*—Diverse students benefit from the expertise of teachers who know about the first language (L1) needs of students. In order to provide for both the language needs and the disability, it will be necessary to engage in discussion with an ELL teacher. In some schools this may be an English as a second language (ESL) teacher, or there may be a bilingual teacher, bilingual interpreters, or a cultural liaison who can assist with home language. The ELL professional will be able to help you understand the "silent" stage, when ELLs are processing language, as distinct from a speech language impairment. Your responsibility is to distinguish between characteristics of a disability and the academic language needs and social language comprehension of ELLs.

Identify and Use Collaborative Practices

Throughout this book, several references have been made regarding the increasing diversity of United States classrooms, and that this diversity is not limited to large urban schools. Diversity in language and culture is found in schools of all sizes in urban, sub-urban, and rural communities. Most teachers will experience diverse language and culture classrooms. The scope and sequence of the teaching strategies and learning activities required to meet the educational needs of students in diverse classrooms is truly extensive.

One way schools are meeting this increasing challenge facing teachers is to initiate collaborative teaching situations. As previously defined, collaboration is the process where two or more individuals *systematically plan, design, instruct, assess, and evaluate student educational goals.* In a collaborative teaching situation, special education teachers and general education teachers work together to implement instruction in a teaming format. By doing so, they share instructional responsibilities and accountability for student progress.

Collaborating With the General Education Teacher

There are several factors that support effective collaboration between the special education teacher and the general education teacher.

Common Planning Time

First of all, in order to have a successful collaboration the teachers need to have planning time together. This is commonly achieved in one of two ways:

1. The special education teacher's preparation times are aligned with their general education partner's preparation times at least once per week.

2. The school administration ensures that release or compensated time is scheduled for teaching pairs to work together on a regular basis.

However, just because preparation times are common, does not guarantee teachers will appropriately use the time. To ensure that collaborative planning occurs, the school administration may require the participation of all teaching teams in planning and reflection time. In addition, the school administration should also provide the teaching pair with support and guidance for how to use their common planning and reflection time.

Proximity

Another important factor in a successful collaboration has to do with location. This may mean that the special education teacher's office and/or teaching space is located close to their general education partners' classroom. Special education teachers are provided with space as needed in the classroom where they are coteaching.

Resources

Available and appropriate resources are also required to support a successful collaboration. Special education teachers must be provided with the general education curriculum material needed for planning and instruction. These generally include textbooks, teacher's manuals, standards, and other instructional articles, assignments, and worksheets. Special education teachers also need to have equal access to classroom teaching tools such as boards, bulletin boards, paper, markers, charts, and models.

Many schools want to support collaboration efforts and maximize special education services. Professional license requirements, teaching experience, and the number of students on IEPs are some of the considerations districts take into account when determining collaborative practices.

Collaborative Instructional Process

Planning for effective instruction with a collaborative teaching partner frequently requires a great deal of patience, communication, and negotiation.

Define Learning Objectives

Effective instructional planning often begins with clearly defining the students' learning objectives. These may be content objectives, language objectives, behavior objectives, and/or other suitable learning objectives. It is vitally important that both team members, according to their expertise, contribute to the determination and specificity of these learning objectives.

Select a Collaborative Teaching Model

The selection of the collaborative teaching model should support the students' achievement of the targeted learning objectives. There are several collaborative teaching models from which to select. Each has advantages and limitations. The most common collaborative teaching models include the following:

• *Station Rotation*—Collaborating teachers assist students as they rotate through two or more learning stations. Each collaborating teacher might stay at different specific locations (such as new instruction or a station with specialized equipment), or rotate with a specific group of students. Stations could be focused on instructional items such as review, discussion, experiments, creations, research, technology, assessment, multimedia projects, or journal entries.

• *Team Teaching*—Collaborating teachers share the teaching aspects of the lesson. In this model, teachers can take turns (turn teaching) with various components of the lesson, or teachers can blend their instruction together (interactive teaching) throughout the lesson.

• *Alternative Teaching*—Collaborating teachers divide the class into two groups. Groups could be the same size or one could be larger than the other, depending on the lesson's learning objectives and the specific needs and/or abilities of students. Each collaborating teacher is responsible for a specific group. Teachers could switch groups during the lesson.

• *Support Teaching*—One of the collaborating teachers (either the special education teacher or the general education teacher) is the lesson's primary teacher. The other teacher supports the instructional process by observation or drifting/floating throughout the classroom. The supporting teacher helps students by checking on their work or by merely observing students to determine how their learning is progressing in areas such as behavior, speaking, note taking, and questioning.

The teaching model that is selected should also be supportive of each collaborating teacher's instructional strengths. Collaborating teachers should vary their instructional responsibilities over the course of several lessons. For example, one teacher should do the class introduction and focusing activity on one day and the other teacher should do the introduction and focusing activity on the next day. Other instructional practices should also be rotated as determined by teacher interest and expertise.

Negotiating Instructional Preferences

In addition to determining the best teaching model for the targeted learning objectives, collaborating teachers must have forthright discussions and come to a consensus on several other components of the instructional process. These include:

1. Noise/Movement
   a. How will we decide the acceptable noise level for various classroom activities?
   b. How will we decide the acceptable level of student movement for various classroom activities?

2. Homework
   a. How much homework should the students have?
   b. Will it be a different amount for different students?
   c. How often should homework be given?

3. Grading
   a. How will the students be assessed, evaluated, and graded?
   b. Who will have this responsibility?
   c. Will the responsibility be shared?
   d. How and who will monitor student progress?

4. Classroom Management
   a. How can collaborating teachers be consistent in dealing with students' classroom behavior?
   b. Is one teacher more responsible than the other in terms of classroom behavior management?
   c. What are the critical areas (such as procedures and routines) needed for consensus? These may include behaviors such as what to do when entering and leaving the classroom; turning in completed assignments; going to the locker, nurse, office, or restroom; making up missed work, sharpening a pencil, or asking for help.

5. Lesson Materials
   a. What materials are needed for the lesson?
   b. Who is responsible for getting those?

c. Are there any special classroom set-up requirements (like seating, bulletin boards, technology)?

6. Using L1

a. How will we decide if it is appropriate for students to use their primary or home language (L1) in a language-diverse classroom?

b. If it is appropriate for student to use L1, how will we decide under which circumstances it is appropriate?

7. Lesson Schedule

a. How important is it to stick to the lesson schedule?

b. If students offer several comments during the lesson, should the lesson's progress be delayed to the next day or should student comments be discouraged to assure the lesson is completed as scheduled?

8. Parent

a. What type of communication should the collaborating teachers have with parents?

b. Who should do that?

c. How often?

9. Effectiveness

a. How will we assess and evaluate the effectiveness of our collaborative lesson?

b. How will we assess and evaluate the effectiveness of the curriculum?

10. Administrative Support

a. How will we approach the school/district administration to seek collaboration support?

b. How can we be proactive in meeting with other collaborating teachers to discuss successes and challenges?

Collaborating With Others

Educational success for students with disabilities depends on the commitment of many individuals. For most special education teachers, collaboration involves working closely with paraprofessionals and extends beyond the school to collaborate with community partners and parents.

Paraprofessionals

In special education, a paraprofessional is an important collaborating partner. The paraprofessional is an adult hired to support a student with disabilities. Sometimes the paraprofessional is called a paraeducator, educational assistant, or teacher's aid. The relationship that develops between a paraprofessional, a student, and a teacher is a unique partnership. It can be complex to direct the work of a paraprofessional as well as coordinate instruction and ensure compliance.

A paraprofessional brings distinct skills to the job but will also need specific training in how to manage, motivate, document, observe, conduct assessments, or provide academic support. A paraprofessional may provide a cultural perspective or a community connection. The paraprofessional is often in a position to bring details about the student's day into a discussion. Mutual respect, trust, and open communication are key ingredients in the partnership between a paraprofessional and a teacher. By promoting the professional growth of a paraprofessional, you will encourage the development of a collaborative environment.

You can reinforce skills necessary for a paraprofessional by:

- identifying, requesting, or providing specialized training that may be required when working with a student;
- clearly identifying expectations;
- establishing routines;
- listening to concerns;
- modeling confidentiality; and
- encouraging input and ideas.

In addition to collaborating partners in schools, there are individuals outside of school who will become involved in collaboration.

Community Partners

Health professionals (doctors, community health nurses, mental health workers), probation officers, vocational rehabilitation counselors, employers, and human or social service personnel may be among the community partners you meet with on a regular basis. When working with community partners, be well prepared to describe the characteristics of the disability and how that disability impacts daily life for the student. Use examples to help explain. The collaboration required in these out-of-school situations is different than the classroom model but no less important.

1. Scheduling will be more complicated. It may take longer to arrange common times.
   a. Identify yourself and your role.
   b. Leave clear and concise messages.
   c. Identify hours when are you available.
   d. Give a direct phone line where you can be reached at the school after hours or leave your cell phone or home number.
   e. Ask for meeting times that would be convenient for the other person.

2. Individuals in private practice are guided by other funding mechanisms. It may dictate the amount of time they are available to meet or provide service to the student.
   a. Be specific about the goal for the meeting.
   b. Clarify the service you want the professional to provide.

3. Make sure you understand the professional terminology used by others. Provide others with details related to the special education terms you use.

4. Ensure confidentiality.

5. Provide or seek parental approval documentation that allows you to share student information with the community partner.

6. Follow up.
   a. Define the goals.
   b. Determine who is responsible.
   c. Establish timelines.

7. Assess the outcome.

In reviewing the components of collaboration between special and general education teachers, it is apparent that many of the effective steps and strategies can be used with community partners. The physical or professional boundaries may be more defined but the need to communicate, problem solve, and use professional expertise to address needs of students remains the same.

Collaborating With Families

Working with parents as partners is another ingredient in strengthening the educational network for students with disabilities. The life of a family in the twenty-first-century family is complex. Family dynamics revolve around adult and child interactions in single or two-parent homes; surrogate, foster, GLBT, or blended families; or in homes where grandparents or extended family members are raising children. Parents or guardians are challenged to find time, resources, and energy amid the demands associated with a disability.

Parents cycle through a number of emotions including guilt, fear, sadness, anger, ambivalence, joy, and optimism. Every day and each developmental stage can bring a new set of circumstances for parents. The way parents cope with a child's disability may depend on the age of the parents, the number of children and birth order in the family, the severity of the disability, the support network available, and the age of onset or identification of the disability.

Parents can take on any of the following roles:

- *Allies*—Parents and teachers working together can reinforce each other. They can identify resources or reinforce academic and behavioral programs outside of the school setting.
- *Advocates*—Parents generally know and can tell you what the needs of the child are. Their knowledge and expertise is necessary when developing a plan to benefit their child.

- *Autonomous*—Some parents appear to be disengaged and independent of the process. This doesn't mean they are not interested. It may be a sign of respect for authority or it may be one way they have learned to survive.
- *Aggressive*—A parent may be outspoken and forceful. This may be a reaction to past experiences where "fighting" for service for the child was the norm.
- *Avoidant*—Sometimes parents deny or defer acting on the knowledge about their child with a disability. It may be the result of anger or fear of the consequences.

It's important to use practices that reinforce effective communication and positive relationships with parents.

- Seek out parents' knowledge without judging.
- Welcome their expertise and show you value their input.
- Show respect for the unique backgrounds and cultural or religious practices of the family.
- Focus on the strengths of the family.
- Look for opportunities to engage the family in the educational process.
- Offer to teach specific practices the family can reinforce at home such as listening to the child read.
- Be honest and sensitive at the same time.

It is sometimes necessary to identify support that may be needed by the family. In doing so, stay focused on how family intervention helps meet the students' educational goals.

Enhancing Collaboration—Friendly Reminders

Novice special educators typically rate themselves high on the collaboration scale at the beginning of a year. That confidence can be challenged as the year progresses. Developing and maintaining a positive attitude, implementing collaborative instructional practices, negotiating classroom differences, and eliminating role ambiguity of team members will be effective in reducing barriers. Collaboration is a continuous process and requires proactive strategies to prevent challenges from becoming obstacles. Other ideas to open doors and encourage collaboration include the following:

Be Visible

As more importance is placed on access to curriculum, the need for strong liaisons between teachers is critical. It is tempting to stay cloistered away trying to write reports, but new special educators should connect with classroom teachers whenever possible.

Use Jargon Judiciously

Special education is notorious for using complex terminology, acronyms, and jargon. For persons outside of special education, many of the words and abbreviations tend to sound too medical, too legal, or too confusing. Help reduce the stress and create a "user-friendly" work environment that encourages collaboration.

- Consider opportunities to clarify terms whenever possible.
- Be proactive.
- Serve as a resource for information.
- A personal contact engages other staff in an ice-breaking and informative discussion about the various roles and responsibilities associated with special education.
- Begin immediately to develop and disseminate a list of special education words. Create a list that is specific to students on your caseload. This practice has many benefits. It provides evidence you are knowledgeable, organized, and interested in assisting others who work with students on an IEP. Table 9.2 provides an example.

Coordinate and Prepare for Meetings

In some cases, general education teachers have not been involved in developing the IEP requirements that they must address in the classroom. Reasons given by classroom teachers for not attending IEP meetings vary. Common excuses and positive responses you can use are given below:

Excuse: What meeting? I didn't know there was a meeting.

Response: Make sure you send the official *Notice of a Team Meeting* document provided by the district.

Excuse: I wasn't invited.

Response: Review the list to include all meeting participants who work with the student.

Excuse: I don't read e-mails.

Response: Use multiple methods as a reminder. Place a follow-up notice in the teacher's mail box, stop by their classroom and offer a friendly reminder, call, leave a voice or text message.

Excuse: I don't look in my school mailbox.

Response: Send an e-mail or use another option as a follow-up reminder.

Excuse: Meetings take too long.

Response: Use an agenda. Follow a structured format. Bring all documents with you.

Excuse: I had no advance notice.

Response: Ten days is the typical advance notice requirement for an IEP meeting.

Table 9.2 Justified Jargon

Acronym	Special Education Term
ASD	Autism Spectrum Disorder
BIP	Behavior Intervention Plan
CDC	Centers for Disease Control
DCD	Developmental Cognitive Delay
ELL	English Language Learner
FC	Facilitated Communication
GE	General Education
HI	Hearing Impairment
ICC	Interagency Coordinating Council
JDC	Juvenile Detention Center
KWL	Know, Want to know, Learned
LV	Low Vision
MA	Medical Assistance
NRT	Norm-Referenced Test
OHI	Other Health Impaired
PLEP	Present Level of Educational Performance
QWERTY	Typical keyboard layout for assistive technology
ROM	Range of Motion
SEAC	Special Education Advisory Council
TDD	Telecommunication Device for the Deaf
UDL	Universal Design for Learning
VR	Vocational Rehabilitation
WS	Waivered Services
X-AM	eXamine All Motives—Functional Behavioral Assessment
YTP	Youth Transition Program
ZPD	Zone of Proximal Development

Excuse: I coach (have childcare, another job, car pool) before or after school.

Response: As best you can, coordinate the schedules of parents and others who are required to attend, and arrange the meeting after you have checked participants' schedules.

Excuse: I don't get paid overtime.

Response: When possible, and if appropriate, arrange IEP meetings during the school day.

Excuse: I don't know the child. The student is not in my class.

Response: This may be a child the teacher will be getting and input will be critical.

Many of the above excuses could be eliminated by being proactive. Early on, when considering the meetings you need to schedule, ask classroom teachers to be specific in identifying hours available for meetings. In a quick e-mail, ask if the entire prep period is open for a meeting, or if there are 15, 20, or 30 minutes at the beginning or end of the period that would be better for meeting. The more specific your questions, the better information you get. Request confirmation of e-mails and ask that responses be returned by a specific, identified date. When the response date arrives, follow up if you have not heard from the teacher. You may not be able to eliminate all excuses, but you can incorporate practices that ensure you are following protocol in preparation for a meeting.

Recent changes in IDEIA (2004) have also addressed some concerns often voiced about IEP meetings and may reduce time commitments for school staff. These revisions include the following:

- Members of the IEP team can be excused from all or some of the meeting if the parent and school agree attendance is not required because the meeting is not related to the curriculum area or related service provided;
- If the curriculum area or related service is being discussed, the IEP meeting can still be held even though the individual is not there if that person has been excused by the parent and school, and if the individual provides written input into the development of the IEP prior to the meeting; and
- Alternate means of conducting meetings or participation by IEP team members, such as using conference calls or video conferencing, is allowed.

When there are issues related to IEP meetings, speak individually with teachers to resolve concerns. Some individuals will not respond regardless of your best attempts. Following procedures and working to accommodate individuals who should be involved in the meeting is evidence of a good faith effort. In some situations, it may be helpful to talk to a mentor or administrator to seek solutions.

Create a Summary of an IEP for a General Education Setting

Many general education teachers confess they have no idea what to do with students on IEPs. Some special education teachers attempt to include a student with disabilities in a general education setting without talking to the classroom teacher. That is a recipe for disaster. In other situations, special educators fail to communicate what methods of instruction or what materials are most appropriate for students on IEPs. By creating a Summary of an IEP for a General Education Setting (Figure 9.1) some problem situations can be avoided.

Figure 9.1 Summary of IEP for a General Education Setting

Student:	ID #:
Grade:	Date:
Teacher(s):	Class:

Goals: *(Specific to the class)*

Curricular or Instructional Strategies/Accommodations Required:

Test-Taking Needs:

Behavior or Management Needs:

Request Books and Assignments

Special education teachers are expected, according to the Council for Exceptional Children (CEC) Standards, to "possess a solid base of understanding of the general content area curricula, i.e., math, reading, English/language arts, science, social studies, and the arts sufficient to collaborate with general educators in: teaching or coteaching academic subject matter content of the general curriculum" and be able to design "appropriate learning and performance accommodations and modifications." (CEC, 2009). No Child Left Behind also supports the concept of access to learning and high-quality teaching.

Regardless of the disability or grade level, if a student on an IEP is in a general education class, special education teachers are in a position to better assist the student and collaborate more effectively if the student books and assignments are available in advance. Special educators who have the teacher's edition of the curriculum have been much more effective in preteaching content, developing students' skills, and supporting students in the content area. Many collaboration efforts fail because assignments and books are not shared between teachers.

Principals can support collaboration by ensuring funds are available for purchasing the additional book(s) for students and a teacher's guide for the special education teacher at each appropriate grade level. IEP teams can reinforce this accommodation by writing the needs statement to include the general education classroom text and preteaching or reteaching of assignments, as necessary.

SUMMARY

Successful collaboration is supported administratively, planned thoughtfully, implemented with student achievement in mind, and assessed for effectiveness. As a new special educator, it is helpful to identify individuals who will be involved in specific collaborative situations. Reflect on personal attributes, roles and responsibilities, and helpful practices in preparing to collaborate. Prioritize work with teams in order to stay focused on student learning.

SELF-ASSESSMENT AND REFLECTION

After reading Chapter 9, please reflect on your knowledge and skill.

Self-Assessment Items

Respond to the following by answering Yes, Somewhat, or No.

I am able to

_____ 1. Identify attributes of successful collaborators;

_____ 2. Describe roles and responsibilities in collaborative teams;

_____ 3. Identify and use collaborative practices when working with general education teachers, families, and others;

_____ 4. Use practices that enhance collaboration.

Reflection

1. Which of the self-assessment items do you feel fully competent in?

2. Which of the self-assessment items do you feel need some more work, emphasis, or study time?

3. Identify two specific actions that you can take to enrich and strengthen your instructional effectiveness.

Conclusion: Wrapping Up, Reflecting, and Celebrating!

Teaching students with disabilities is not without challenges; some are big challenges, many are small challenges. On the other hand, knowing you taught a student to read, to use technology, to maintain socially appropriate behaviors, or to be more independent offers immeasurable rewards. It's thrilling to have a student thank you for helping him or her learn something new. The student's appreciation may be given as a smile, through sign language, or in written or electronic form. The thanks you receive can come immediately, in a few days, and sometimes years later.

The goal of this book is to enable the special education teacher to experience more rewards than challenges. Unfortunately for teachers, there is no magic instructional strategy that works for all students all of the time. However, there are instructional practices, teaching strategies, and student learning activities that can provide a higher likelihood of student learning, achievement, and success.

Chances are your classroom will be very diverse. Today's students come to the classroom with many languages, cultures, customs, learning preferences, and learning abilities. Chapter 1 helped the teacher be better prepared for those diversities. Organizing a classroom for the best instructional and learning environment is a critical component associated with learning success. Chapter 2 suggested ways the classroom and work could be structured. Classroom management related to student behavior is a universal concern for teachers. Chapter 3 offered approaches to promote positive behaviors and reduce or eliminate disruptive behaviors while at the same time complying with special education requirements.

A well-designed instructional lesson provides students with efficient and effective learning opportunities. Chapters 4, 5, and 6 presented ideas about planning and implementing well-designed, quality lessons. Lesson plans, active student learning, and the multitude of ways to enhance student learning through the use of graphic organizers were described.

Educational technology is advancing at lightning speed. Chapter 7 highlighted current technology and ways to support the teacher's instructional practices. In years ahead, teachers are bound to see unimaginable classroom technology become a reality.

Assessment and evaluation are critical components in every classroom. The obvious connection to assessment and evaluation is the student. To what degree did the student meet his or her educational goals? Teachers gather (assess) "lots" of student information and then, based on that information, make a professional judgment (evaluation). Chapter 8 offered several ways to help the teacher make decisions about assessment and evaluation issues. And, as a friendly reminder, assessment and evaluation issues should also be applied to the curriculum, the classroom environment, and instructional practices.

The final chapter, Chapter 9, illustrated partnerships and roles designed to support student achievement. In some cases, law requires team involvement, but more often districts are voluntarily implementing collaboration. In many cases, it is the special education teacher who is responsible for initiating the collaborative team.

An efficient and effective special education program does not happen spontaneously. Granted, some instructional aspects such as budget and caseload are typically out of the special educator's direct decision-making authority. However, detailed and conscientious planning can result in comprehensive practices that will boost not only student learning but your confidence, competence, and connections to the profession.

Congratulations! You are growing more knowledgeable of the profession and of diverse needs of students. Just for fun, you can review chapter objectives and at the same time, complete this chart.

Numeral	English	Spanish	Hmong
1			ib
2		dos	
3	three		
4			plaub
5		cinco	
6	six		
7	seven		
8		ocho	
9			cuaj

References

Artiles, A. J., & Trent, S. C. (1994). Overrepresentation of minority students in special education: A continuing debate. *The Journal of Special Education, 27*(4), 410–437.

Assistive Technology Act of 1998. USC PL105-394. Retrieved January 13, 2010, from http://www.section508.gov/docs/AT1998.html.

Baca, L., & Amato, C. (1989). Bilingual special education: Training issues. *Exceptional Children, 56*(2), 168–173.

Baker, P. H. (2005). Managing student behavior: How ready are teachers to meet the challenge? *American Secondary Education, 33*(3), 51–64.

Bellanca, J. (2007). *A Guide to Graphic Organizers* (2nd ed.). Thousand Oaks, CA: Corwin.

Bergs, M. (2005). *Working with English language learners.* Mankato, MN: Limited Liability Corporation.

Berliner, D. C. (1986). In pursuit of the expert pedagogue. *Educational Researcher. 15*(7), 5–13.

Billingsley, B. (2005). *Cultivating and keeping committed special education teachers.* Thousand Oaks, CA: Corwin.

Bloom, B. S., Engelhart, M. D., Furst, E. J., Hill, W. H., and Krathwohl, D. R. (1956). *Taxonomy of educational objectives: The classification of educational goals. Handbook 1: Cognitive Domain.* New York: Longman.

Bolt, S. E., & Thurlow, M. L. (2004). Five of the most frequently allowed testing accommodations in state policy. *Remedial and Special Education, 25*(3), 141–152.

Boys Town Education Model. (1970). *Using preventative teaching to teach social skills.* Boys Town, NB: Boys Town Press. Retrieved January 11, 2010, from http://www.parenting.org/parenting-tips/social-skills

Bransford, J., Brown, A., & Cocking, R. (Eds.). (2000). *How people learn: Brain, mind, experience, and school.* Washington, DC: National Academy Press.

Brownell, M., Adams, A., Sindelar, P., Waldron, N., & Vanhover, S. (2006). Learning from collaboration: The role of teacher qualities. *Exceptional Children, 72*(2).

Cardona, G. (2005). World Book Multimedia Encyclopedia (Version 10.01) [Computer software]. The Software MacKiev Company.

Carlson, E., Brauen, M., Klein, S., Schroll, K., & Willig, S. (2002). *Study of personnel need in special education.* Rockville, MD: Westat Research Corporation. Retrieved December 8, 2005, from http://www.ecs.org/html/offsite.asp?document=http%3A%2F%2Fwww%2Espense%2Eorg%2F+

Carnahan, C., Musti-Rao, S., & Bailey, J. (2009). Promoting active engagement in small group learning experiences for students with autism and significant learning needs. *Education & Treatment of Children, 32*(1), 37–61.

Castellani, J. D., & Jeffs, T. (2001). Reading and writing: Teaching strategies, technology tools, and the Internet. *Teaching Exceptional Children, 33*(5), 60–67.

Center for Applied Special Technology. (2010). *Universal design for learning.* Retrieved September 29, 2008, from http://www.cast.org/teachingeverystudent/.

Council for Exceptional Children. (1993). Code of ethics. *CEC Policy Manual,* retrieved Feb. 8, 2009, from http://www.cec.sped.org/Content/NavigationMenu/AboutCEC/CECsMissionand Vision/default.htm.

Council for Exceptional Children. (2003). *What every special educator must know: The international standards for the preparation and certification of special education teachers* (5th ed.). Reston, VA: Council for Exceptional Children.

Council for Exceptional Children. (2008). *What every special educator must know: Ethics, standards, and guidelines for special educators* (6th ed.). Arlington, VA: Author. Retrieved Oct. 14, 2009, from www.cec.sped.org.

Council for Exceptional Children (2009). *What every special educator must know: Ethics, standards, and guidelines for special educators* (6th ed.). Retrieved January 12, 2010, from http://www.cec.sped.org/Content/NavigationMenu/ProfessionalDevelopment/Professional Standards/?from=tlcHome.

Crawford, V. M., Schlager, M. S., Penuel, W. R., & Toyama, Y. (2009). *Supporting the art of teaching in a data-rich, high-performance learning environment.* Retrieved August 17, 2009, from http://ctl.sri.com/publications/displayPublication .jsp?ID=485.

Donovan, M. S., & Cross, C. T. (2002). *Minority students in special and gifted education.* Washington, DC: National Academy Press.

Duany, L., & Pittman, K. (1990). *Latino youths at a crossroads.* Washington, DC: Children's Defense Fund.

DuFour, R. (May, 2004). What is a "professional learning community?" *Educational Leadership, 61*(8).

Edds, D. (2002). Technology for special educators: How the Web and some wooden blocks are changing the life of a boy. *School Planning and Management, 41*(6), 76–77.

Elliot, J. (2007). Providing academic support for teachers and students in high-stakes learning environments. *Journal of Applied School Psychology, 23*(2), 27–107.

Emmer, E. T., & Stough, L. M. (2001). Classroom management: A critical part of educational psychology, with implications for teacher education. *Educational Psychologist, 36*(2), 103–112.

Espin, C. A., & Yell, M. L. (1994). Critical indicators of effective teaching for preservice teachers: Relationships between teaching behaviors and ratings of effectiveness. *Teacher Education and Special Education, 17,* 154–169.

Flannery, M. E., (January/February, 2009). Born in the USA: A new look at America's English language learners, *NEA Today, 27*(4), 24-29.

Friend, M. & Cook, L (2007). *Interactions: Collaboration skills for school professionals* (5th ed.). Boston: Pearson.

Friend, M., & Bursuck, W. (2009). *Including students with special needs: A practical guide for classroom teachers (5th ed.).* Boston: Allyn & Bacon.

Galanti, G. A. (1991). *Caring for patients from different cultures.* Philadelphia: University of Pennsylvania Press.

Gardner, H. (1983). *Frames of mind.* New York: Basic Books.

Gay, G. (2002). Culturally responsive teaching in special education for ethnically diverse students: Setting the stage. *International Journal of Qualitative Studies in Education. 15*(6), 613–629.

Gerlic, I., & Jausovec, N. (1999). Multimedia: Differences in cognitive processes observed with EEG. *Educational Technology Research and Development, 47*(3), 5–14.

Goldstein, L. (2003). Disabled by paperwork. *Education Week, 22*(38), 1–23.

Goldstein, A., & McGinnis, E. (1997). *Skillstreaming the Adolescent: New strategies and perspective for teaching prosocial skills.* Champaign, IL: Research Press.

Hallenbeck, M. J. (2002). Taking charge: Adolescents with learning disabilities assume responsibility for their own writing. *Learning Disabilities Quarterly, 25,* 227–246.

Harry, B., & Klingner, J. K. (2005). *Why are so many minority students in special education? Understanding race and disability in schools.* New York: Teachers College Press.

Hasselbring, T. S., & Glaser, C. H. W. (2000). Use of computer technology to help students with special needs. *Future of Children, 10*(2), 102–122.

Higher Education Opportunity Act (2008), USC PL110-135, s 24 A B. US Government Printing Office. Retrieved January 13, 2010, from http://frwebgate.access.gpo.gov/cgi-bin/getdoc.cgi?dbname=110_cong_public_laws&docid=f: publ315.110.pdf.

Hinds, M. (2002). *Teaching as a clinical profession: A new challenge for education.* New York: Carnegie Corporation.

Horvath, L. S., Kampfer-Bohach, S., & Kearns, J. F. (2005). The use of accommodations among students with deaf-blindness in large-scale assessment systems. *Journal of Disability Policy Studies, 16*(3), 177–187.

Individuals With Disabilities Education Improvement Act. (2004). IDEIA [IDEIA 2004, 20 U.S.C. ss 1414 (d)(I) et seq.] Washington, DC: Government Printing Office.

Individuals with Disabilities Education Improvement Act (2004). USC PL108-446. Retrieved January 9, 2010, from http://www.nichcy.org/Documents/reauth/PL108-446.pdf.

Individuals with Disabilities Education Act Amendments (1997). USC PL105-17. Retrieved January 10, 2010, from http://www.ed.gov/policy/speced/leg/idea/idea.pdf.

Ingersoll, R. M., & Smith, T. M. (2003). The wrong solution to the teacher shortage. *Educational Leadership, 60*(8), 30–33.

Inspiration Software, Inc. (2003). *Graphic organizers: A review of scientifically based research.* Retrieved September 1, 2009, from http://cf.inspiration.com/download/pdf/SBR_summary.pdf.

Kraus, L. E., Stoddard, S., & Gilmartin, D. (1996). *Chartbook on disability in the United States, 1996* (An InfoUse Report). Washington, DC: US Department of Education, National Institute on Disability and Rehabilitation Research. Retrieved January 10, 2010, from http://www.infouse.com/disabilitydata/.

Lowdermilk, J., Fielding,C., Mendoza, R., Garcia de Alba, R., & Simpson, C. (2008). Selecting English language acquisition technology. *Technology in Action 3*(2).

Lynch, E. W., & Hanson, M. J. (1999). *Developing cross cultural competence* (2nd. ed.). Baltimore, MD: Paul H. Brookes Publishing.

Maag, J. W. (2001). Rewarded by punishment: Reflections on the disuse of positive reinforcement in schools. *Exceptional Children, 67,* 173–186.

Maheady, L., Michielli-Pendl, J., Mallette, B., & Harper, G. F. (2002). A collaborative research project to improve the academic performance of a diverse sixth grade science classroom. *Teacher Education and Special Education, 25*(1), 55–70.

Mainzer, L., Castellani, J., Lowry, B., & Nunn, J. (2006). GLOBE tech: Using technology to maximize classroom performance with team-based instruction. *Technology in Action, 2*(1).

Meyer, C. R. (1996). Medicine's melting pot. *Minnesota Medicine, 79*(5), 5.

Mid-continent Research for Education and Learning. (2000). *What works in classroom instruction.* Retrieved September 18, 2009, from http://www.mcrel.org/Newsroom/hottopicInstruction.asp.

National Center for Culturally Responsive Education Systems. (2002). *Determining appropriate referrals of English language learners to special education: A self-assessment guide for principals.* Washington, DC: National Association for Bilingual Education.

National Center for Education Statistics. (2003). *Young children's access to computers in the home and at school in 1999 and 2000.* Washington DC: US Department of Education.

National Center on Universal Design for Learning. (2009). *Three primary principles guide UDL—and provide structure for the guidelines.* Retrieved September, 23, 2008, from http://www.udlcenter.org/aboutudl/udlguidelines.

National Education Association (1975). Code of Ethics, Washington, DC: National Education Association. Retrieved February 8, 2009, from http://www.nea.org/home/30442.htm.

National Educational Association. (2006). *Research spotlight on recruitment and retention.* Retrieved February 23, 2009, from http://www.nea.org/tools/16977.htm.

No Child Left Behind Act (2001). USC PL 107-110 s 2401 (d). *Enhancing Education Through Technology (E2T2).* Retrieved January 10, 2010, from http://www.ed.gov/policy/elsec/ leg/esea02/pg34.html.

Ogunwole, S. U. (2002). The American Indian and Alaska Native population: 2000. *Census Brief:* US Census Bureau, 1. Retrieved February 8, 2009, from http://www.ncd.gov/newsroom/publications/2003/native_toolkit.htm.

Oliver, R. M., & Reschley, D. J., (December, 2007). Effective classroom management: Teacher preparation and professional development. *Connection Issue Paper: Improving Student Outcomes in General and Special Education.* National Comprehensive Center for Teacher Quality (NCCTQ). Retrieved January 12, 2008, from http://www.tqsource.org/topics/effectiveClassroomManagement.pdf

Ortiz, S. (2004). *Comprehensive assessment of culturally and linguistically diverse students: A systematic, practical approach for nondiscriminatory assessment.* Retrieved October 1, 2005, from www.nasponline.org/resources/culturalcompetence.

Otis-Wilborn, A., Winn, J., Griffin, C., & Kilgore, K. (2005). Beginning special educators' forays into general education. *Teacher Education and Special Education, 28*(3/4), 143–152.

Paneque, O., & Barbetta, P. (2006). Study of teacher efficacy of special education teachers of English language learners with disabilities. *Bilingual Research Journal, 30*(1), pp 171-193. Retrieved March 13, 2010 from http://docs.google.com/viewer?a=v&q=cache:W-3_Bo0fvtQJ:citeseerx.ist.psu.edu/viewdoc/download%3Fdoi%3D10.1.1.119.6305%26rep%3Drep1%26type%3Dpdf+Bilingual+Research+Journal+2006Study+of+teacher+efficacy+of+special+education+teachers,+Paneque+and+Barbetta&hl=en&gl=us&pid=bl&srcid=ADGEESi_YFT4xDPXORS9xGFLGQ0qzBT1ow7MrVEEtAoMbma6QC5e2nBaGPF5LuPveaPPAw1nfZs4HnCD-QVT9N4J52Jut8t1DD62JPWCKYpx470JH4wKXBl7CeJaWKjd9YMcRgh81yVs&sig=AHIEtbQJx-IXGdO6STQ6oYieeaGF7XI8Yg

Parette, H. P., Wojcik, B., Peterson-Karlan, G., & Hourcade, J. J. (2005). Assistive technology for students with mild disabilities: What's cool and what's not. *Education and Training in Developmental Disabilities, 40,* 320–331.

Prensky, M. (2001). Digital natives, digital immigrants. *On the Horizon 9*(5).

Rohwer, J., & Wandberg, R. (2001). Creating and implementing "robust" learning tasks. *American Journal of Health Education, 32*(4), 248–251.

Rohwer, J., & Wandberg, R. (2005). Improving health education for ELL students in the mainstream classroom. *American Journal of Health Education, 36*(3), 155–164.

Rosa, L. (1973). Helping students solve problems: The "SODAS" method. Retrieved January 12, 2010, from http://www.pki.nebraska.edu/studentinfo/simp/mentoring_guide/SODAS%20Text.pdf.

Salend, S. (2009). Using technology to create and administer accessible tests. *Teaching Exceptional Children, 41*(3), 40–51.

Salend, S., & Duhaney, L. M. (2002). Grading students in inclusive settings. *Teaching Exceptional Children, 34*(3), 8–15.

Samway, K., & McKeon, D. (1999). *Myths and realities: Best practices for language minority students.* Portsmouth, NH: Heinemann Publishing.

Scott, T. M., Liaupsin, C., Nelson, C. M., & McIntyre, J. (2005). Team-based functional behavior assessment as a proactive public school process: A descriptive analysis of current barriers. *Journal of Behavioral Education, (14),* 57–71.

Serfass, C. & Peterson, R. (2007). A guide to computer-managed IEP systems. *Teaching Exceptional Children, 40*(1), 16–21.

Sheldon-Wildgen, J., Sherman, J. A., Schumaker, J. B., & Hazel, J. S. (1981). *ASSET: A social skills program for adolescents.* Champaign, IL: Research Press.

Sprick, R., Garrison, M., & Howard, L. H. (1998). *CHAMPS: A proactive and positive approach to classroom management.* Eugene, OR: Pacific Northwest Publishing.

Stiggins, R. J. (2001). The unfulfilled promise of classroom assessment. *Educational Measurement: Issues and Practice, 20*(3), 5–15.

Stodden, R. A., Galloway, L. M., & Stodden, N. J. (2003). Secondary school curricula issues: Impact on postsecondary students with disabilities. *Exceptional Children, 70,* 9–25.

Thompson, S., & Thurlow, M. (2001). State special education outcomes: A report on state activities at the beginning of a new century. Minneapolis: University of Minnesota, National Center for Educational Outcomes. Retrieved January 10, 2010, from http://www.eric .ed.gov/ERICDocs/data/ericdocs2sql/content_storage_01/0000019b/80/ 29/cb/4c.pdf.

Thurlow, M., Albus, D., Shyyan, V., Liu, K., & Barerra, M. (2004). *Educator perceptions of standards-based instruction for English language learners with disabilities* (ELLs with Disabilities Report 7). Minneapolis: University of Minnesota National Center on Educational Outcomes. Retrieved March 13, 2010 http://www.cehd.umn.edu/NCEO/OnlinePubs/EllsDisReport7.html

Thurlow, M., Elliot, J., & Yselldyke, J. E. (2003). *Testing students with disabilities: Practical strategies for complying with district and state requirements.* Thousand Oaks, CA: Corwin.

Trent, S. C., & Artiles, A. J. (1998). Multicultural teacher education in special and bilingual education. *Remedial and Special Education,19*(1), 2–6.

US Department of Education. (2006). *Child Count.* Office of Special Education Programs. Washington, DC: US Government Printing Office.

US Department of Education, National Center on Education Statistics. (2008). *The condition of education 2008.* Washington, DC: US Government Printing Office.

US Department of Education, Office of Special Education Programs. (June, 2002). Local administrator's role in promoting teacher quality. *Study of Personnel Needs in Special Education* (Summary Sheet). US Department of Education, Office of Special Education Programs. Retrieved June 9, 2008, http://ferdig.coe.ufl.edu/spense/administratorsummary.pdf.

US Department of Labor (1991). *What Work Requires of Schools: A SCANS Report for America 2000,* xvii-xviii. Department of Labor: US Government Printing Office. Retrieved May 30, 2008, from http://www.ncrel.org/sdrs/areas/issues/methods/assment/as7scans.htm.

Walker, H., Todis, B., Holmes, D., & Horton, G. (1988). Adolescent Curriculum for Communication and Effective Social Skills (ACCESS). Austin, TX: Pro-Ed Publishing.

Wehmeyer, M. L., Agran, M., & Hughes, C. (2000). A national survey of teachers' promotion of self-determination and student-directed learning. *The Journal of Special Education, 34*(2), 58–69.

What Works Clearinghouse. (2008). US Department of Education, Institute for Education Sciences, Retrieved August 8, 2008, from http://ies.ed.gov/ncee/wwc/.

Whitaker, S. D. (2001). Supporting beginning special education teachers. *Focus on Exceptional Children, 34*(4), 1–18.

Will, M. C. (1986). Educating children with learning problems: A shared responsibility. *Exceptional Children, 52,* 411–415.

Zaballa, J. (October, 1995). The SETT framework: Critical areas to consider when making informed assistive technology decisions. Closing the Gap Conference on the Use of Assistive Technology in Special Education and Rehabilitation, Minneapolis, MN.

Zehler, A. M., Fleishman, H. L., Hopstock, P. J., Stephenson, T. G., Pendzick, M. L., & Sapru, S. (2004). Descriptive study of services to limited English proficient (LEP) students and LEP students with disabilities. Arlington, VA: Development Associates.

Zehr, M. A. (2004). Report updates portrait of LEP students. *Education Week, 23*(18), 3.

Zhao, Y., Pugh, K., Sheldon, S., & Byers, J. (2002). Conditions for classroom technology innovations. *Teachers College Record, 104*(3).

Index

CORWIN

A SAGE Company

The Corwin logo—a raven striding across an open book—represents the union of courage and learning. Corwin is committed to improving education for all learners by publishing books and other professional development resources for those serving the field of PreK–12 education. By providing practical, hands-on materials, Corwin continues to carry out the promise of its motto: **"Helping Educators Do Their Work Better."**